CUISINE of CULTURE

REVISED

PART TWO

Published by:
The Professional Image, Inc.
In the US: South Beach and South Florida
International: St. Croix, St. Thomas, Tortola
Contact us at: foodbrat@gmail.com

ISBN: 978-1-6664-1513-1
"Culture of Cuisine" ~ Revised

Thanks to our Staff:
SENIOR Editor: Eileen Clark
ASSISTANT EDITOR: JESS "E"
Photographers: The Professional Image, Inc.

Copyright © 2025 by Michael Bennett ~ the FoodBrat ! All rights reserved.

No part of this publication may be reproduced, distributed, or transmitted in any form or by any means, including photocopying, recording, or other electronic or mechanical methods, without the prior written permission of the publisher, except in the case of brief quotations embodied in critical reviews and certain other non-commercial uses permitted by copyright law. For permission requests, write to the publisher, addressed "Attention: Permissions Coordinator," at the address below:

The Professional Image, Inc.
~South Florida~
96401 Overseas Hwy. | Key Largo, Fl. 33037
305.799.8305

Ordering Information:

Quantity sales: Special discounts are available on quantity purchases by corporations, associations, and others. For details, contact the publisher at the address above.

Orders by U.S. trade bookstores and wholesalers. Please contact TPI

a Dedication:

From our past, our heroes of Cuisine:

A TRIBUTE AND TIME LINE TO THOSE THAT MADE MIAMI AND SOUTH FLORIDA COOKERY A HOUSEHOLD WORD....

THIS TIME LINE SHOULD GIVE AN IDEA OF WHEN SOME OF OUR FAMILIAR VETERAN CHEFS FIRST CAME UPON THE STAGE -- AND IF/WHEN THEY OPENED A PLACE OF THEIR OWN.

1986: ALLEN SUSSER OPENS *CHEF ALLEN'S* IN AVENTURA. *James Beard recognition: Chef Allen is nominated for a James Beard Award for Best Chef in the South, signaling national attention and acclaim.*

1986: DEWEY LOSASSO GAINS NOTICE AS CHEF OF THE *FOUNDLINGS CLUB* IN MIAMI BEACH.

1995: Dewey is awarded the prestigious title of Best Chef in Miami by Miami New Times and is recognized by Bon Appétit as one of the Top 10 Emerging Chefs in America.

1988: MARK MILITELLO OPENS *MARK'S PLACE* IN NORTH MIAMI BEACH.

1995: Mark Militello is named Best Chef in Florida by Miami New Times, and Mark's Place gains recognition from Bon Appétit, Gourmet, and Food & Wine Magazine. He is widely regarded as one of the top chefs in the United States at the time.

1989: DOUG RODRIGUEZ SPARKS NUEVO LATINO CUISINE AT *YUCA* IN CORAL GABLES. *(which stands for "Young, Unconventional, Creative, and Artistic") a pioneering restaurant that would become synonymous with Nuevo Latino Cuisine. The concept blends traditional Latin American and Caribbean flavors with modern techniques and creative presentation, signaling a revolution in Miami's culinary scene.*

1989: PASCAL OUDIN TURNS HEADS AS CHEF OF THE COLONNADE IN CORAL GABLES. *Over the late 1980s and early 1990s, he worked as executive chef at top-tier Miami institutions such as Dominique's and the Grand Bay Hotel's Grand Café, refining his skills under French culinary legends including Alain Ducasse, Roger Vergé, Joseph Rostang, and Gaston Lenôtre .*

1991: NORMAN VAN AKEN COMES TO MIAMI AT *A MANO* IN THE BETSY ROSS HOTEL ON OCEAN DRIVE. *This was a pivotal moment for South Florida cuisine. Van Aken brought his bold, globally inspired "New World Cuisine" to Ocean Drive. 1995: Launches Norman's in Coral Gables—the flagship project that cements his reputation as the region's fusion cuisine pioneer.*

Published Works - *Feast of Sunlight (1988) earlier*

- *The Exotic Fruit Book (1995)*
- *New World Kitchen (2003)*
- *My Key West Kitchen (2012, co-authored with son Justin)*
- *No Experience Necessary: The Culinary Odyssey… (2013)*
- *My Florida Kitchen (2017)*

1993: JONATHAN EISMANN BRINGS *PACIFIC TIME* TO A STILL-UNDEVELOPED LINCOLN ROAD. *2008 Eismann relocates Pacific Time to the emerging Miami Design District, re-imagining the restaurant with a fresh, more casual small-plates format. The menu now features Mediterranean and Asian flavors with much lower prices and greater variety.*

1994: ROBBIN HAAS MAKES THE NEW *COLONY BISTRO* ON OCEAN DRIVE THE HOTTEST SPOT IN TOWN. *Within months, Food & Wine recognized him as one of "America's Best New Chefs," and his bold, South Florida–infused menu earned praise from Gourmet, Esquire, and the James Beard Foundation — all cementing his status in the celebrated "Mango Gang" of visionary Miami chefs.*

1994: JAN JORGENSEN'S *TWO CHEFS* DEBUTS IN SOUTH MIAMI. IT IS STILL THERE. *2024, Jan co-authors A Cook's Table with wine journalist Todd Wernstrom, a richly illustrated cookbook and wine-pairing guide featuring over 125 recipes drawn from his career and personal culinary journey.*

1994: CINDY HUTSON AND DELIUS SHIRLEY OPEN *NORMA'S ON THE BEACH* ON LINCOLN ROAD, THE PRECURSOR TO *ORTANIQUE* ON THE MILE. *1999 – Opening of Ortanique on the Mile in Coral Gables. 1997 they launched Ortanique on the Mile in July 1999.*

1994: MICHAEL SCHWARTZ CO-LAUNCHES *NEMO* IN SOUTH BEACH. 2007: *Re-emerging in the Design District,*

Schwartz opened Michael's Genuine Food & Drink, grounded in local sourcing, seasonal ingredients, and a "genuine" philosophy.

2000: MICHELLE BERNSTEIN GETS LOTS MORE ATTENTION AT *AZUL* IN THE MANDARIN ORIENTAL. *Azul was one of the first restaurants in Miami to receive major accolades, earning a James Beard nomination for Best Chef: South. The restaurant became known for dishes that showcased her commitment to local, seasonal ingredients, and creative yet refined presentations.*

2003: ANDREA CURTO- RANDAZZO AND FRANK RANDAZZO DAZZLE WITH *TALULA* ON SOUTH BEACH. *Talula garnered numerous accolades, including Best New Restaurant and a AAA Four Diamond Rating, and Andrea was featured as a Food & Wine Best New Chef in 2000 for her earlier work at Wish Restaurant. Andrea appeared as a contestant on Season 7 of Bravo's Top Chef (Washington, D.C.), raising her national profile as a creative, grounded chef willing to showcase her Southern Italian–inspired cooking.*

....a TRIBUTE TO SOUTH FLORIDA CHEFS

I invite you to embark on a journey—a journey through daily competition, struggle, and moments of grandeur.

As any chef will tell you, "***This is the hardest job I've ever loved.***" For most of us, it's true. Being a chef is not for the faint of heart. Culinarians are a unique breed—people who take raw ingredients and transform them into art, often under the harshest of conditions.

There are days when the path of a chef feels unsettling, chaotic even, and some will never fully understand the magnitude of what we do. But those who do, know this:

*It is the turmoil that drives us forward.
*It is the heat and the frustration that recharge us.
*It is the never-ending, often daunting expectations that push us toward perfection.
*It is the absence of culture surrounding us that makes us want to carve, weave, and shape edible masterpieces as if conducting a Mozart-like symphony.
*It is the lack of understanding from others that makes us want to teach, to share the depths of our craft.
*And it is the infinite possibilities of creation that fuels our need to strive for a singular vision of excellence.
*Innovation is not born overnight.
*It arises over time, sculpted by countless hours of trial and error, experimentation, and refinement.
*It's in the daily grind, the relentless pursuit of perfection, where true culinary artistry is shaped.

Our Introduction:

The Evolution of Modern Cuisine on the New American Riviera

In America, modern cuisine is in a constant state of evolution. Innovation is the lifeblood of every successful chef. To innovate is to craft ideals—an intricate and demanding process. When a chef creates a cuisine, it begins as a thought, evolves through finesse, then enters production, and finally reaches refinement. Cuisine has always been both a temporary and contemporary art form, requiring chefs to continuously pursue new levels of creativity.

This book is inspired by the imaginative contributions of South Florida chefs, past and present. It is written for both emerging culinary talents and experienced professionals who are eager to push boundaries and redefine what is possible in the kitchen.

Modern cuisine is not a fixed style—it is a mindset. It's the act of recognizing your culinary limits and then moving beyond them. On the New American Riviera—a vibrant and diverse region of South Florida—there are no rigid culinary boundaries. This is a place of experimentation and reinvention, where the only rule is creativity. Here, cuisine is not linear. It flows endlessly, shaped by labor, imagination, and cultural fusion.

Learning the art of cooking is a deeply sensory and repetitive experience. It is not something that can be fully grasped by reading instructions alone. Instead, mastery comes through consistent repetition—through practice, mistakes, refinements, and more practice. This hands-on learning is the foundation of true culinary discipline.

In South Florida, inspiration often begins at the market. As chefs wander through open-air stalls filled with tropical produce, their minds drift—imagining bold combinations and new flavors. This kind of creative daydreaming is essential. It allows chefs to build flavor profiles that honor the past, while moving beyond outdated culinary conventions. Recipe development should always tell a story—one rooted in place, culture, and personal experience. For me, that story is told through the lens of South Florida's locally harvested tropical foods, which reflect the tastes and traditions of our community.

This is the hallmark of a cuisine born on the New American Riviera.

Like musicians drawing from the foundational chords of classical compositions, chefs use the time-tested techniques of French Classical cuisine as a springboard for innovation. From there, we create something fresh, vibrant—sometimes even avant-garde. Before a recipe is written, a chef must first taste the dish in their mind. This mental tasting draws from years of sensory memory and countless hours of experimentation. It's how we refine what I call a taste-variance—a harmonious blend of ingredients that reveals something new, surprising, and memorable.

That moment when someone takes a bite and says, "Ah-ha, that's what the sauce was missing!"—that's what we strive for. Taste-variance is the pursuit of balance and brilliance in flavor, often discovered through a process that's equal parts science, artistry, and intuition.

Chefs are not only creators; we are also caretakers. Like raising children, our recipes must be nurtured, guided, and refined over time. Repetition brings efficiency, accuracy, and confidence. Through practice, steps are streamlined, and our intuition for seasoning and balance becomes second nature. Writing recipes that others can replicate exactly as intended is a reflection of that dedication. This is a chef's artistic responsibility—to document, to refine, and to inspire through precise communication.

Recipe creation is trial by fire—pun intended—and healing a flawed dish is just as much an act of artistry as it is one of perseverance. To be a chef is to commit to the daily practice of innovation, to create with care, and to continually push the boundaries of flavor and form.

Welcome to the New American Riviera—
a place where cuisine is alive, ever-changing, and always reaching for the next evolution.

FLORIDA,

a culinary Wasteland or Dreamland...

This excerpt is rich with vivid descriptions and passionate insights into the evolution of "New World Cuisine" in South Florida. If you're looking to "refine or modernize" this text for a book, article, or promotional use, here's a "streamlined and professional rewrite" that maintains your voice and expertise, while improving flow, grammar, and clarity:

"South Florida's Culinary Awakening: The Rise of New World Cuisine"

A few decades ago, no one would have questioned what Florida was best known for—sunshine, oranges, and bikinis. But since the 1990s and the emergence of New American Regional Cuisine—what we now call "New World Cuisine"—Florida has earned its place on the national culinary map.

Along the vast, coconut tree-lined coastline of South Florida, a vibrant culinary evolution has taken hold. This new style of cooking has not only redefined local cuisine—it has surpassed all the food traditions that came before it.

As the sun crests over the horizon, South Beach—or SoBe, as locals call it—comes alive. Some are still winding down from a long night of dancing, while others are just beginning their day basking in golden rays. Film crews prepare for another sunrise shoot, and parrots squawk from the palms above. It's a new day in what has become known as the "New American Riviera". And just as the sun brings light to the city, "New World Cuisine brings fresh energy and bold innovation to the plate."

This cuisine is built on energy—visually, culturally, and gastronomically. It reflects the "diverse influences of South Florida's five foundational culinary cultures": Native American, Old Southern, Latino, Caribbean, and Asian. These traditions have been fused into a spirited, innovative food culture unique to this region.

At the heart of every plate is a "locally sourced superstar ingredient", often something exotic and rarely seen in mainstream American kitchens. These might include tropical fruits like "mamey, lychee, longan, starfruit, jackfruit, sapodilla, atemoya", or "canistel", and root vegetables like "malanga, cassava, name, and boniato".

A typical dish might feature "grilled Yellowtail snapper"—a nod to Native cooking—topped with a "mango and Scotch Bonnet salsa" inspired by Caribbean and Latin traditions. Drizzled over this is a ""coulisgrette"", a fusion of coulis and vinaigrette, made from local fruits like "atemoya" and "canistel". Alongside it sits a "malanga dumpling", stewed in an "Asian-style lemongrass broth". Every element represents a convergence of technique, flavor, and culture—a harmonious blend that couldn't exist anywhere else.

What sets this cuisine apart is its “um-replicable “taste-variance””—a layered, vibrant profile that’s possible only in South Florida’s subtropical climate. These fruits and vegetables can’t grow in colder states, and that makes the culinary creations of this region truly one-of-a-kind. And, then there’s the “abundance of seafood”—a coastal bounty that is hard to match. The waters off South Florida teem with local species: “Atlantic swordfish, mahi-mahi, yellowtail snapper, wahoo, pompano, groupers, and multiple varieties of jacks, mackerels, and tuna.”

Together, these land and sea ingredients form the foundation of a cuisine that is not only “geographically specific”, but “globally inspired”. South Florida’s New World Cuisine is more than a trend—it’s a movement that reflects the cultural mosaic and culinary ambition of a region redefining what it means to be American.

The Inland Harvest: A New Frontier of South Florida Cuisine”

Beyond its sun-drenched coastline and seafood bounty, South Florida’s culinary identity continues to evolve thanks to the growing popularity of what I call the ““inland and farm-rose” foods”—a collection of wild, foraged, and locally farmed provisions from Florida’s interior.

Groups like the “Seminole Indians” and other specialty harvesters provide chefs with rare and regionally significant ingredients: “venison, wild turkey, boar, hare, quail, alligator, frog legs, bass, striped bass, perch, trout, catfish, crayfish”, and even “heart of palm” (also known as *swamp cabbage*). These ingredients may seem exotic to outsiders, but in Florida, they represent a rich, sustainable food culture rooted in the land.

This melding of the exotic and the everyday has elevated many local ingredients into “true culinary superstars”. Just as France has distinguished culinary regions like Lyon and Burgundy, “South Florida is carving out its own identity in American regional cuisine”.

The South Florida Twist: The Art of Balance in the Kitchen

A daily paradox for South Florida chefs is to strike a balance between “tropical exuberance” and “palate comprehension”—to honor both flavor and familiarity in each plate presentation.

Take, for example, an acidic sauce crafted from ingredients like “Key lime juice, calamondin, or citrus vinegar”. When paired with a fatty, flavorful fish such as “Seabass”, this sauce does more than brighten the dish—it “balances richness” and enhances the eating experience. Fats are not just flavor carriers; they trigger the brain’s response to satiety. When they coat the receptors in your stomach, it sends a message to your brain: “I’m full.” In truth, your stomach isn’t full—your receptors are simply “coated in richness”.

This is the "yin and yang" of cooking in South Florida. Imagine a "crisp citrus cookie"—sharp with orange zest—cradling a silky "atemoya custard". Or a sweet, creamy "Cambodian mango" contrasted with the fiery heat of a "Scotch Bonnet pepper" in a salsa or chutney. These are the moments when flavors and textures dance across the plate—and across cultures.

Chefs here have learned to blend culinary traditions and cooking applications to "layer textures", "elevate flavors", and "challenge perceptions".

"Discovering a Culinary Wonderland"

Once you understand how common ingredients interact—how fat balances acid, or how heat plays against sweetness—you unlock the door to integrating lesser-known foods into your recipes. Suddenly, a tropical root vegetable or an obscure fruit isn't intimidating—it's an opportunity.

We judge what's new by what we already know. When chefs dare to experiment with the unknown, they tap into the "culinary wonderland that is South Florida"—a region where culture, climate, and creativity converge to inspire every plate.

Mango Mania:

The Sweet Soul of the Teflon City

What makes "Teflon City" —as South Beach has come to be known—such a singular place? It's not just the sun or the style. It's that South Florida is fearlessly, fashionably different, especially in its food scene.

This is evident in the explosion of new restaurant concepts, particularly those centered around seafood and Pan-Asian fusion. These menus reflect the cultural kaleidoscope of South Florida, and one ingredient has risen to iconic status: the "mango".

Once considered exotic, the mango is now as familiar in the South Florida pantry as apples are elsewhere. The region's chefs have embraced this tropical fruit with such enthusiasm that it has inspired an "international celebration of taste, texture, and creativity".

The Mango Festival: A Celebration of the King of Fruit
Each July, the "Fairchild Tropical Botanic Garden" in Coral Gables hosts the "International Mango Festival"—the largest event of its kind in the Western Hemisphere. Fairchild is home to over "130 varieties of mango", curated by "Dr. Richard Campbell", who travels the world collecting rare mango species and cultivating them in South Florida's uniquely suitable climate.

Dr. Campbell leads a panel of "celebrity chefs" in a culinary showcase that draws mango lovers and foodies from across the globe. One highlight is the "Horizontal Mango Tasting"—akin to a horizontal wine tasting—where attendees sample and compare several mango varieties at the same stage of ripeness. Each fruit is explored for its "flavor profile, texture, acidity, sweetness, aroma, and culinary versatility".

In contrast, the "Vertical Tasting" features a single variety of mango presented at "various stages of ripeness"—from green and tangy to fully ripe and decadently sweet. This progression offers insight into the fruit's evolving characteristics and possible culinary applications throughout its life cycle.

From Bathtubs to Notebooks: Mango Culture Gets Juicy

"I've been doing this event with Dr. Campbell for five years," one local chef shares, "and every year the audience gets more passionate. You'd think we were giving away secrets to eternal youth." One year, South Florida celebrity chef "Robbin Haas" stole the show with his cheeky take on mango indulgence, suggesting the best way to eat one is "naked in the bathtub."

It's not just playful commentary—attendees are "serious mango connoisseurs". They take meticulous notes as chefs describe the "flavor, fragrance, texture", and even the ""sexy" characteristics" of each mango. One chef recounted a story of his wife trying to check the time on a neighbor's watch, only for the neighbor to "shield her tasting notes", suspecting espionage. "These folks aren't just fans—they're "mango-a-holics",he laughed. "They're ready to offer up a virginal sacrifice for our mango cooking tips."

The King of Fruit, Crowned in South Florida.

There's no doubt: South Florida has adopted the "mango as its culinary crown jewel". From high-end kitchens to backyard trees, from chutneys and salsas to cocktails and sorbets, the mango is more than just a fruit—it's a symbol of the region's "bold fusion cuisine", "cultural diversity", and "irrepressible spirit".

.

In South Florida,
Mango isn't just eaten—it's celebrated.

Table of Contents

PART ONE:

Chapter One:

Culture and Cuisine:

Bringing a talent to bear that develops something unique!
Breaking it down into the most elemental levels:
"Culture" is thought...
And, an innovation forms, it becomes your relentless culinary formula. As a Chef, you have to your taste buds as a guide to correctness.

A community's "Culture" is a Stage where your "Cuisine" is the Limelight which accentuate your ideals and theories.

Here's a professionally refined and cohesive rewrite of your latest piece, ideal for use in a "culinary memoir", "cookbook introduction", or "editorial feature". It keeps your heartfelt message, culinary insight, and distinctive voice while polishing grammar, organization, and tone.

The Culture of Cuisine:

Forged by Sweat, Styled with Soul. South Florida's cuisine isn't just cooked—it's crafted. It rises from heat, humidity, and history, where kitchens pulse like drumbeats and ingredients arrive sun-kissed and sea-salted. This is a food born of sweat—of chefs leaning over blazing grills, fishermen dragging in the morning's catch, farmers coaxing tropical fruit from stubborn soil. It's shaped by tears, too—the tough lessons of trial and error, of bold ideas that sometimes burn before they shine.

But above all, South Florida's cuisine is styled with soul. It is the food of migration and mingling, where Caribbean spice rubs shoulders with Latin fire, where Old World traditions are re-imagined under new skies. It is not static, but restless—an evolving art form, always experimenting, always tasting, always reinventing.

To cook in South Florida is to carry on a hot style of American cuisine that is as much about place as it is about flavor. It is food that knows no borders, food that reflects the rhythms of the streets and the tides, food that dares to be tropical, modern, and deeply personal all at once.

This "Culture of Cuisine" is the transformation of raw ingredients into something more than nourishment—it's a "reflection of identity", shaped by each chef's personal vision of what food can be. Here, cookery is not static—it is a process of experimentation, of listening to ingredients and allowing them to suggest direction, of balancing tradition with daring. It is cuisine shaped by care: care for the integrity of the product, care for the craft of presentation, and care for the community who gathers to share it.

In South Florida, culinary technique meets cultural storytelling. Each dish becomes a dialogue between past and present, between migration and belonging, between refinement and spontaneity. What results is not only sustenance, but a living art form—an evolving chapter in America's culinary identity, both rooted in place and expansive in imagination.

One of the chefs I interviewed for this book once told me, "recipes are like children." You guide and shape them through every stage of life, offering structure when they need discipline, freedom when they are ready to grow, and attention when they begin to speak in their own voice. That responsibility transforms a cook into something more than a technician. A true chef becomes a concept curator—someone who not only prepares food, but cultivates ideas, nurtures identity, and carries forward the narrative of a cuisine.

Through this lens, cookery ceases to be a fixed set of instructions and becomes instead a living discipline. Recipes evolve with time, adapting to new influences, new climates, new migrations. They carry memory but also embrace experimentation, intuition, and care. They are shaped by culture as much as by craft, and in their evolution they reflect the growth of both people and place.

South Florida's cuisine exemplifies this truth. It is alive with transformation—restless, inventive, and deeply rooted in the rhythms of its community. Here, culinary technique meets cultural storytelling, and every plate becomes not only nourishment, but a testament: that food, like people, is capable of becoming more than it was yesterday.

A Regional Identity, Rooted in Place.

Across the varied neighborhoods of South Florida, cuisine may shift in style, but certain trends unite us. Diners crave "healthy seafood options", "locally sourced produce", and menus that reflect the region's biodiversity and bold character. With more than "1,000 miles of coastline", seafood naturally anchors our plates—and our palates.

As the culinary world moved beyond the butter-and-cream-heavy traditions of decades past, Florida chefs embraced a fresher, brighter thesis. Today, our kitchens are filled with "fresh herbs, extra-virgin olive oil, tropical fruits, capsicum heat", and the creative use of alternative ingredients to meet dietary needs—gluten-free, dairy-free, nut-free. This evolution is not just about flavor—it's about "inclusion", "innovation", and honoring the needs of the modern diner.

"How Was Our Cuisine Crafted?"

To understand how South Florida's cuisine emerged, we must look beyond ingredients. It's not only what's on the plate—it's the "rituals, relationships, and histories" that surround the food. It's the story of "when, where, how, and with whom" we dine. Our culinary identity is a fusion of tropical harvests, sea-based ingredients, and time-honored techniques that have been locally refined.

Cuisine is one of the most "powerful markers of cultural distinction". Since America's first printed cookbook—""American Cookery" in 1796"—chefs and food lovers have sought to define what American food truly is. For generations, critics wondered: "Does America even have a culinary identity?"

Today, the answer is a resounding yes.

Since the 1980s, "American regional cuisine" has taken root and flourished. From coast to coast, local styles have emerged, shaped by geography, climate, and community. And South Florida has "risen from overlooked to celebrated", evolving into a "distinctive culinary powerhouse".

From Overlooked to Iconic: South Florida's Culinary Renaissance.

Not long ago, South Florida was considered little more than a culinary afterthought. While the dining cultures of New York, San Francisco, and Los Angeles were celebrated as the nation's benchmarks, this region was quietly dismissed. Even the Michelin Guide—long regarded as the global arbiter of gastronomic excellence—paid South Florida scant attention.

The reason was clear: our menus once leaned heavily on convenience rather than creativity. Too often, kitchens relied on frozen fish hauled from distant oceans, prefabricated crab cakes shipped in from industrial suppliers, and bland fillets of imported whitefish that bore no connection to our own waters. The food was serviceable, but it was disconnected—disconnected from place, from story, and from soul.

What followed, however, was nothing short of a renaissance. As chefs began to reject imitation in favor of authenticity, they turned to the bounty of their own backyard: snapper and grouper still shimmering from the Gulf Stream, spiny lobster pulled from the Keys, mangoes, papayas, and avocados ripened under subtropical sun. They brought with them the culinary traditions of the Caribbean, Latin America, and beyond, fusing technique with intuition, heritage with experimentation.

South Florida, once overlooked, has become iconic—a stage where cuisine is not only consumed but celebrated, a hot style in America's ever-evolving culinary story.
But that began to change in the 1980s. Florida chefs started to embrace their surroundings and turn to "local ingredients": "Key West stone crab, Lake Okeechobee alligator", and of course, the "Key lime pie".

By the mid-1990s, South Florida wasn't following food trends —we were "setting them".

Gone were the temperate-climate staples like fiddle-head ferns or sun-dried tomatoes. In their place came vibrant new flavors: "cilantro, mango, Scotch bonnet peppers", and locally caught "Gulf grouper". Imagine a wood-fired "Florida pompano with crushed pecans and citrus", finished with a mango or passionfruit "coulis-grette". These aren't just dishes—they're declarations of identity.

A Culinary Culture Defined by Discovery

South Florida's cuisine has been "officially recognized as a regional phenomenon", one of the hottest culinary movements of the 1990s—and it continues to evolve. Today, our food culture stands as a "testament to creativity", a "celebration of diversity", and a "model of reinvention".

It is a culture born from heat and history, spiced by heritage, and served with heart. And it continues to inspire chefs, delight diners, and reshape the way America—and the world—defines cuisine.

Chapter Two

Understanding Food...
Understanding the Relationships of Ingredients

The Destiny of Ingredients: Art, Science, and the Voice of a Chef.

Some ingredients are destined to be together.
The aromatic trio of "scallion, ginger, and garlic" is to Asian cuisine what "mirepoix"—the French combination of onion, celery, and carrot—is to European tradition. South Florida chefs recognize that certain ingredients have an inherent "harmony", whether by cultural tradition or culinary intuition.

Yet at times, the destiny of an ingredient is to be celebrated "on its own", untouched and unmasked, allowing the diner to savor its "pure essence". Both pairings and simplicity have their place in the kitchen, and a chef must know when to choose each path.

We see this harmony in many global staples. The Mediterranean's "garlic, tomato, and basil" is as classic as it is comforting. Or consider the Caribbean and Latin American staple: "sofrito"—a paste of stewed onion, garlic, peppers, and herbs, used to deepen the base of sauces, soups, and stews. Or think of the endless riffs on salsa, from tomato to mango to papaya, each grounded by lime juice, jalapeños, cilantro, and onions.

The lesson: many ingredient combinations are “naturally complementary”. Discovering your own signature blend—one that makes you glad you became a chef—is the foundation of your culinary identity.

“Signature Through Experimentation”

A chef’s journey is one of “culinary daydreams and recipe reinvention”. Let your ideas evolve. Let the trends of the time inform your experiments. The movement toward healthier cooking brought new techniques. The rise of sustainability ushered in local sourcing. And the next innovation—whatever it may be—should inspire us to reevaluate and refine once again.

The line between “art and science” in food is vanishing. Walk through any modern grocery store and you’ll see labels filled with chemical enhancements, preservatives, and laboratory-engineered flavorings. The modern family is shopping in a landscape shaped as much by food chemistry as by tradition.

That’s why chefs have a responsibility to “return to nature”. To seek out the best—"fresh, local, responsibly raised ingredients”—and to support those who grow and raise them. It’s not a trend—it’s a revival of how the world’s greatest cuisines always functioned. And yes, local farmers are now being paid fairly for the quality they bring to the table, making the entire supply chain stronger.

“Food as Art, Chefs as Storytellers”

“Food is art.” And presentation is its frame.

The garnish, the plate, the visual balance—it all adds “perceived and real value” to the dish. But there’s more. The “story” of the food—how it was discovered, what inspired it, how it’s meant to be savored—transforms a dish from nourishment into “narrative”.

That’s why “writing matters”. Print out your brain. Keep a notebook. Write down ideas, define flavor profiles, tweak ingredients to reflect your personal palate. Test, refine, and then share. Because if you’re the only one who understands the recipe, it will never reach the audience it deserves.

Every great dish begins as an idea. That idea becomes an ideal. And when written well, it becomes a “legacy”.

Modern Recipe Writing: Speaking to a New Audience”
Today’s recipe readers are more informed than ever. They’re not just home cooks—they’re “television cooking show viewers”, “Instagram explorers”, “TikTok tasters”. They expect clarity, creativity, and personality.

Modern chefs must write for a “diverse and informed audience”. Gone are the days when cookbooks were only for newlyweds learning to cook hearty meals. Today, readers want “flavor stories”, cooking science, cultural background, and dietary adaptability. Describe “why” a recipe matters.

Share the process of its creation. And don't be afraid to make it "distinctively yours".

Chef Norman Van Aken once built a new genre of "New World Cuisine" from this very method: taking unfamiliar tropical fruits, describing them vividly, and preparing them using familiar Latin-American cooking techniques. In doing so, he eased diners into the unknown—and introduced a new culinary language to America.

"Your Culinary Voice Must Be Heard"

......Your "ideals define your identity" as a chef. But if no one hears them, they won't matter.

Today, chefs must also be "communicators and marketers". Identify who you're speaking to. Research where your audience gets their information. Partner with food writers, press agents, influencer's, and publishers. Study how press releases are structured. Learn from articles that made an impact. Then, "do it yourself".

Use free press release platforms. Seed the web with your voice. Create media that "positions you as the expert"—not just in recipes, but in passion, purpose, and point of view.

Don't wait to be discovered. Make it impossible to ignore you. When media outlets begin to reference you, restructure that content and build on it. Let it lead to new opportunities. The more your voice is heard, the more your restaurant—and your career—become “synonymous with excellence”.

“The Chef’s Legacy: Influence and Recognition”

This process may feel self-promotional. But it’s not ego—it’s strategy. The chefs I know who’ve secured lasting careers all understood that “reputation is power”. With the support of great publicists, restaurants thrive. And chefs gain the recognition that inspires staff, draws diners, and builds legacies.

Even the most inspired dish won’t change lives -- if no one knows about it.

“Your “cuisine is your voice”. Your menu is your manifesto. And your career is your canvas”.

Chapter 3

The Culture of Cuisine:

A Legacy Forged in Fire and Flavor

"Like-minded thoughts bring forth a common culture."
The bond between chefs is enduring—rooted in a shared pursuit of excellence, creation, and connection.

""Artists will be artists"," regardless of the medium. I've found that if chefs weren't creating art with food, they would be painting, sculpting, or composing in other forms. Culinary artists belong to a community in constant search of outlets for their creativity—driven by the need to "satisfy others through deeply personal, carefully honed cookery."

While some pursue the limelight, most chef-artists I know do it for something more profound: "the enrichment of others". To feed is to give. And to give joyfully, day in and day out, is what defines our culture.

"The First Three Steps: Listen, Read, Write"
Let me take you on a journey—one filled with daily competition, sacrifice, and magnificence. The life of a chef is a paradox: ""the hardest job I ever loved"," as many of us say.

We are a "rare breed". We take raw materials and transform them into art—often under pressure, in tight quarters, amidst heat and chaos. And yet, we thrive. Because:

* It is "turmoil" that drives us.

* It is the "heat and frustration" that recharge us.

* It is "daunting expectations" that push us to excellence.

* It is the "lack of surrounding beauty" that compels us to create it ourselves.

* It is "what we don't yet know" that urges us to learn.

* It is the "infinite possibility" that sharpens our focus.

"Back to the Future: The Rise of a Regional Cuisine"

Miami is a "sun-drenched, sand-laced epicurean emporium", revered by food lovers across the globe. It's a city shaped by multicultural identity—and our cuisine reflects that perfectly.

To understand the present, we must revisit the past. Since the 1980s, South Florida has been home to a vibrant, genre-defying culinary movement. Its names have shifted—"New World Cuisine, Floribbean, Tropical Fusion, Nuevo Latino"—but its "spirit remains the same".

South Florida chefs rose to national prominence by redefining American cuisine with a distinctly tropical edge. Our culinary expression is based on "fresh Florida seafood", "exotic tropical fruits", and "root vegetables" that offer both bold flavors and health-conscious alternatives.

We moved beyond the blackened-everything era of the 1970s and the gourmet gimmicks of the 1980s. Our chefs broke rules, ignored trends, and created a "culinary thesis of their own", centered on vibrant ingredients and multicultural inspiration.

"A Subtropical Symphony"

What makes our cuisine uniquely South Floridian?

* The sub-tropical climate that allows us to grow fruits like "mango, sour sop, papaya, passionfruit", and "atemoya" year-round.
* A bounty of "local seafood": clams, pompano, Yellowfin tuna, blue crab, shrimp, cobia, dolphin fish (mahi-mahi), grouper, and five regional varieties of snapper including "Yellowtail", "Mangrove", and "Hogfish"—all sweeter and more tender than their northern cousins.
* Grilling over "Florida hardwoods", a nod to ancient Caribbean cookery, now common in our healthier modern kitchens.

And of course, the "endless fusion" with Latin and Caribbean food cultures—St. Maarten, Cuba, Jamaica, Chile, Mexico, Peru, Argentina, Brazil. Each adds a brush stroke to our culinary canvas.

"Mis en Place of a Movement"

Our spice cabinets are filled with "salsas, mojos, rubs, adobos", and tropical herbs drawn from local flora. The "Old World methods" many of us were trained in are reborn through the "New World lens" of exotic ingredients and cultural synthesis.

It's this "mashup of tradition and innovation" that continues to place South Florida's food scene at the forefront of American cuisine.

*"The destiny of nations depends on the manner in which they are fed".Jean-Anthelme Brillat-Savarin (1825)

"Sustenance for the Future"
Something extraordinary happened in South Florida—and it hasn't stopped evolving. A regional food movement was born, and "three decades later", it still pulses with life.

Our people are proud of their heritage. That pride is expressed in "art, music, and most deeply in food". South Florida is home to cultures that share common roots—and cuisine becomes the bridge between them.

As "James Beard" observed, cuisine defines culture just as powerfully as dance, art, or language. Here, in South Florida, "food is identity". It's a shared story told on every plate.

We are chefs. We are artists.
And we are stewards of this culinary culture.

Creativity and South Florida Chefs

In South Florida, culinary techniques are often developed in ways that are characteristically prepared in polar directions. The region in which the cuisine developed might even carry a regional-based namesake. These names give further culinary conceptions a sense of meaningful posture, both locally and globally. This is how the terms "New World Cuisine" and "Caribb-ican" entered our South Florida culinary vocabulary. These terms denote the types of food or the structure of culinary preparation and help diners understand the culinary ideals behind a chef's bill of fare.

Consequently, the Culture of Cuisine in South Florida leans heavily in a Latino direction. What sets a culture apart—and gives it unity—is the richness of its artistic heritage.

Whether It's the Weather...

If a culture is defined by what is eaten, how it's eaten, and when, then South Florida is a Central American assemblage of culinary thoughts and ideals. Our future culinary direction emerges from these heritage-influenced postures.

People in South Florida have dined later in the day for decades. The climate is warm—hot, even—for most of the year. Late dining is common in many equatorial regions for the same reason. Warm weather has greatly influenced what has become popular in South Florida: lighter cuisine, outdoor dining, and menus bursting with healthy, fresh entrees. Promenades lined with pastel-hued buildings invite people to dine al fresco, enjoying meals that reflect both the weather and the culture.

Because our cuisine emphasizes lighter, healthier choices—like seafood and salads—South Florida's cookery stands apart naturally.

Differences are Distinct.

Chefs prepare food in ways that suit their chosen culinary ideals. These ideals mold the process of perfecting a menu's melodic theme. If the kitchen culture is built on innovation, you'll see thrilling culinary adventures unfold between the rim of every plate. If the culture is one of perfection, you can expect refined repetition focused on a singular cookery category.

South Florida chefs always use local foods. Tropically inspired, seafood-heavy menus have spread across the region. Staff are guided to expect and demand these products, prepared in uniquely imaginative ways. This should be the standard everywhere: menus should reflect the area in which a chef lives and works. In New York, that might mean fresh corn and vine-ripened squash. In South Florida, it means local fish, tropical fruits, and warm-weather cooking.

Cuisine Is a Steadfast Progression Toward Perfection

Mastery requires repetition—dozens, even hundreds of times. This structured repetition is the stabilizing factor of cuisine. Consider French Classical Cuisine. Perfected over centuries, it emphasizes unwavering consistency: the same ingredients prepared the same way, over and over.

While South Florida cuisine draws from French Classical teachings, we stretch its elements into something uniquely our own. French techniques provide our footing, but our chefs build outward from them.

"So many of today's techniques were built in the past."
One chef I interviewed put it this way: "Without the concrete footing of French Classical, we would have to reinvent every dish over and over again."

At the Culinary Institute of America, I often heard, "Be quiet when the chef speaks and take plenty of notes."

You never know as much as you think you do. One chef instructor told me:

- "Even if you feel confident after graduation, if you're not learning something new every day, leave and find a place where you can. Then, when you think you've mastered everything, look to the Chinese—they've been cooking for 5,000 years.

"THERE IS SOMETHING TO BE SAID ABOUT TIME.
IT TAKES TIME TO LEARN. IT TAKES TIME TO EVALUATE.
IT TAKES TIME TO FORMULATE YOUR OWN IDEALS.

Mastering a Culinary Thesis.
Mastering a culinary thesis—one you believe in—takes time. Time to replicate. Time to perfect. And time to teach. To pass along a learned ideal to others means allowing them time to absorb it, embrace it, and internalize your philosophy. Mastering a cuisine is, in every way, a matter of time.

Cultivating Ideas
Today's budding chefs have powerful tools at their finger-

tips—namely, the Internet and smart technology. Crossing the culinary universe can now be done with the flick of a switch. Researching, absorbing, and piecing together insights from uncommon sources helps formulate your perfect culinary composition.

Curiosity fuels creativity. Always ask yourself: Is good enough ever enough? The answer should be no. Complacency is creativity's enemy. Remember: tomorrow's culinary classics are yesterday's dreams.

Using today's modern culinary styling is how you build the classics of tomorrow. Just look at spa cuisine and the healthy California movements of the 1980s—they reshaped American cooking. Being on the cusp of culinary trends isn't just good; it's necessary. Defining yourself as a trend leader elevates your expectations and pushes you toward daily improvement. That pressure? That's fuel.

Creativity and Inspiration.

Sometimes a walk on South Beach, a moment near the ocean, or the perfect track on the radio gets my mind turning. Daydreaming is essential for innovation. Surrounded by classical music, I strive for classical perfection. During the dinner rush, I blast Trance or the ripping guitar licks of a 1980s Hair Band. The architecture and rhythm of South Beach fuel my expressive culinary impulses. Exploring the Redlands provides the raw, tropical inspiration I need to innovate.

Innovation comes at different times, from different directions—but it must come. You must always be an ideal pioneer.

Building a Vibe.

The Internet can be your best tool—or your worst nightmare. It saves time, connects people, and spreads your name. But one bad review can follow you forever.

Still, used properly, the Internet lets you create a constant atmosphere of freshness. Posting new dishes, tweaking recipes, and improvising in real time keeps the experience alive for your customers. Start a blog, share your stories, your daily specials, your unexpected inspirations. That sense of creative renewal is what keeps people coming back.

A portion of your clientele wants stability—and that's okay. You can use the Internet to remind them of the excellence they experienced last time, and encourage them to return. In that way, the Internet becomes your best marketing tool.

Trendy restaurants often brand themselves around the idea of change. But trends pass. Remember blackened fish? Gourmet pizzas? Southwestern? California fusion? Even molecular gastronomy is proving to be more of a fad than a foundation. So if your brand is change, make sure your changes improve your menu. Don't change for novelty—change for evolution. You can do this simply. Keep the same protein and switch out the starch, the veg, the marinade, or the sauce. These tweaks don't have to be dramatic, but they should be noticeable.

The Scene Is the Vibe.

The "vibe" can also be the scene that unfolds inside your restaurant. Food, like fashion, is forever evolving. To stay on the cutting edge in food is no different than showcasing your collection at Fashion Week if you're a designer.

On South Beach, the scene is everything. Everyone wants to be seen in the place to be seen. If your restaurant doesn't build a vibe that resonates with the scene, you're already falling behind.

In a breakfast joint, the scene might be a locals-only gem—the kind of place where everyone knows your name. To build that vibe, you have to honor your locals. Make them feel like VIPs. That's where your digital tools come into play: email updates, blog posts, event invites, and photos. Create an ongoing energy that feels spontaneous yet consistent.

What If There Were No Traditions?

What if there were no culinary traditions? Would we be left constantly reinventing the wheel? Probably.

Most chefs of my generation use French Classical cuisine as their foundation. It's our structure. Our road map. The glue that holds our ideas together.

But now we look beyond. We look toward Global cuisine. This modern ideal mixes ingredients, techniques, and flavors from entirely different regions in unexpected ways. It's boundary-pushing, rule-breaking, and wonderfully nontraditional. It's also a reflection of who we are in South Florida: a mosaic of cultures, constantly reinventing ourselves while honoring where we came from. So go ahead—be a trend-setter, a rule-bender, a vibe builder. Let your cuisine reflect your journey, your curiosity, your culture. Because mastering a cuisine isn't just about time—it's about transformation.

Here's a clear, organized, and professionally refined version of your original text. I preserved the voice and core messages while tightening the structure, improving flow, and eliminating repetition and confusion.

Traditional Thoughts: The Layers of Kitchen Heritage.
In one kitchen, I've witnessed three generations of culinary tradition coexisting. Each brings its own flavor—sometimes it's the culture of the restaurant that defines the tradition, and sometimes it's a blend of cookery heritages passed down or picked up along the way.

Take the Caribbean restaurant scene, for example. Caribbean cuisine is rooted in mixture. Colonization by European powers transformed the region's cooking. As islands changed hands between empires, their food evolved—not by erasing the past, but by adapting it to the tastes and systems of each new ruling group. The result is a cuisine layered with African, European, and indigenous influences.

Tradition doesn't vanish; it bends, adjusts, and survives in new forms.

When a chef enters an already established kitchen, they inherit a culinary rhythm they must respect. Any new influence must harmonize with what's already there. For newer restaurants seeking change, that can mean reinventing their heritage. But for restaurants with deep roots, change is harder to swallow. It might take something as drastic as a name change to shift the culinary direction without alienating loyal guests.

Exchanging Ideas and Ideals

There's no better way to explore and refine your culinary identity than working shoulder-to-shoulder with other chefs. I learn every time I step into a friend's kitchen. Watching how someone else builds a dish or communicates with their team can spark something new in your own approach.

Still, there's a difference between exchanging "ideas" and sharing "ideals".

"Ideas" are sparks. They challenge, inspire, and keep us pushing boundaries.
"Ideals" are deeper. They shape the principles behind our food—the why, not just the how.

To truly exchange ideas as equals, chefs must share similar ideals. Without that common ground, the relationship shifts:

one becomes teacher, the other student. Mutual ideals create mutual respect, and that respect is what builds a true peer community—not followers, but members of the same movement.

Ideas drive innovation.
Ideals help us chase it with purpose.

Growing Through Change.

This isn't a call to mimic others. It's a call to stay open. Blinders will only keep you walking the same path, doing the same tired tasks. But cooking is alive, and it evolves.

Working with others lets you challenge your habits. Why must a sauce start with a roux? As gluten-free dining becomes more common, chefs will need new approaches. Tradition doesn't always fit the future. Being a great chef means adapting.

Change doesn't weaken a recipe—it strengthens your creativity. It adds new layers to your culinary skill set. When you revise a technique or rethink an ingredient, you're not abandoning tradition. You're building new ideals on top of old ones. That is how you grow. That's how you stay in this game for the long haul.

Repetition as Foundation.

In my kitchen, repetition is essential. Every chef learns the procedures exactly as I've designed them. Repetition builds muscle memory, consistency, and confidence. Once the fun-

damentals are locked in, then creativity can flourish.
Let me know if you'd like this version tailored for a book chapter, article, blog post, or talk. I can adjust the tone or add visuals and examples if needed.

Kiss...
Keep It Simple Silly

Here's a revised, unified version of your writing—organized for flow, refined for clarity, and edited for rhythm and professionalism. The themes are preserved, but now everything ties together with sharper structure and stronger voice.

The Power of Repetition.
"Repeating the procedure over and over and over is how I train my people to do what I do."

Repetition builds mastery. It simplifies cuisine by refining the process—finding smarter, more efficient paths to the same outcome. Excellence isn't one big trick—it's the dozen small things you do perfectly every day.

Once you master a single step—like achieving perfect taste—you can replicate that across your menu. Repeat a dish enough times and you'll discover ways to make it healthier, more cost-efficient, easier to hold, or faster to serve. When you start cutting wasted steps or unnecessary processes, you gain time, save money, and preserve quality. That's the sweet spot.

After the repetitive work is done,
that's when creativity kicks in.

Modify Your Ideals.
My recipes evolve all the time. My ideals? Not as much. Creating new dishes drives me to revisit and rework older ones with fresh ideas I wouldn't have thought of before. Change isn't always easy—especially when it challenges your core ideals—but sometimes it's necessary to survive. And when that change succeeds? It's one of the most gratifying moments in this craft.

The moment your new approach pays off—when your reshaped ideal proves itself on the plate and in the guest's reaction—you know it was worth it. That's the kind of change that drives me. I know I'm not alone.

The Joy of Simplicity

With repetition, processes become easier—
and simplicity shines.

But simple isn't the same as simplistic. Simplicity in food doesn't mean lack of skill. It means restraint. A bright, clean coulis on a freshly grilled, locally caught grouper is more powerful than any heavy cream sauce or over-reduced jus. Simple food lets ingredients speak for themselves.

I've been cooking this way for years—creating dishes that are clean, ingredient-driven, and uncluttered. Using local foods makes this possible. They're fresher, more vibrant, and the quality shows in every bite.

Of course, cooking with local ingredients also means being ready for surprises. I've got an understanding with my purveyors: if it's the best, I want it. Sometimes, I'll get a box labeled *Special*—my mystery box of the day. It's unpredictable, but it keeps me on my toes. That spontaneity is half the fun of this business.

Texture, Contrast, and the Balance of Opposites

Texture defines a dish.
Soft and crisp. Light and rich. Crunchy and smooth. These opposites play off each other and create dynamic, memorable mouth feel. A dish that balances textures tells the guest that thought went into every element. It speaks for itself.

This is where true cookery lives—not just in flavor, but in the contrasts: hot and cold, sharp and mellow, firm and tender. Take a grilled chicken breast with fruit salsa. Now you've got sweet, sour, warm, cold, crisp, and soft all working in harmony. That complexity becomes a sensory experience.

Define Your Ideas of Cookery: You have to let ingredients speak.

The simpler the preparation, the more clearly the dish communicates. Sometimes bold spices or layered reductions only drown out what nature already perfected. A quick grill might do more to highlight a beautiful vegetable than any sauce ever could.

Taste is only one part of what you serve. Texture, color, temperature—they all shape the experience. A great dish uses contrast to excite the senses and elevate a simple idea into a complete story.

Color, Light, and the Visual Plate.

Color matters. The plate is your canvas.

You might have a perfect dish, but if the colors are dull or poorly arranged, it won't connect. Guests eat with their eyes first. That's why I always say: let the food shine, and use natural light when possible. Especially in photography, natural light makes ingredients pop like no artificial lighting can.

Outdoors, bright tomatoes and fresh herbs explode with color. Inside, artificial light can distort that vibrancy. Balance your plate visually. Use contrasting but natural colors—like the red and green of a Capresse salad—to appeal directly to the senses.

When I edit food photos, I pay close attention to light and shadow. Sharp lines between light and dark help the image print well and add depth. The same applies when plating. Subtle transitions between shades, even pastels softened with cream, guide the diner's eye across the plate—and hint at what's coming next.

Final Thought: Balance Is Everything.

Balance doesn't mean symmetry. It means harmony—of taste, of texture, of color, of temperature. Good food should be deliberate. Every element on the plate should serve a purpose. When your dish tells a story without needing explanation, that's when you know it's right.

What if delicious was easy?

IF DELICIOUS ENTREES WERE SIMPLE
TO MAKE, EVERYONE WOULD HAVE
THEIR OWN TELEVISION COOKING SHOW.

Perceived Value: Cooking Beyond Taste.

As culinarians, we create value through perception. Before a single bite is taken, value is already assigned—through sight, presentation, emotion.

Chefs build this value visually. It's what the customer sees before they taste that earns us our place as artists. Using principles borrowed from design—like the "white space" method—chefs intentionally leave space on the plate. It's not about being minimalist for show. It's about focus. Clean plate. Clean message.

A beautifully plated dish tells the brain: this must taste good. As one of my mentors always said, if the customer sees beauty first, the heart will follow. Win their hearts, and you'll earn their loyalty.

Good food might bring in a guest once. But great food, presented with soul and clarity, brings them back again and again. That loyalty isn't bought with seasoning alone. It's built on emotion, consistency, and visual storytelling.

Food With Soul.

Ask any chef where their passion came from, and many will point to the same place: home.

The soul of cooking often starts with Mom's kitchen or Grandma's apron. Those early memories—family gathered for holidays, meals prepared with care, neighbors stopping by unannounced—shape the heart of a chef.

For many chefs I've spoken with, these roots go deeper. They were raised near farms, where fresh-picked ingredients weren't a luxury—they were the norm. Others, like myself, were raised by the sea, learning that the "soul" of food is tied to its freshness. I still remember learning sushi from an elder Asian chef who taught me: if the fish isn't the freshest thing you can find, don't bother. That principle has stayed with me all my life.

Whether it's farm-to-table or sea-to-sushi, the soul of a dish comes from honoring the ingredient in its purest, freshest form.

Heritage & Innovation: The Caribb-ican Story

Cuisine is never created in a vacuum. It's the product of centuries of influence, trade, colonization, creativity, and resistance. Chinese cuisine spans 5,000 years. In contrast, South Florida's culinary time line is younger, but no less vibrant.

What we now call Caribb-ican cuisine—part Caribbean, part American, all innovation—was shaped by history and migration. Our culinary heritage includes bold tropical flavors, aggressive freshness, and a deeply rooted sense of place.

Many of South Florida's chefs have based their menus on these "Floribbean" roots, fusing Latin, Caribbean, and Southern traditions into something wholly new. But even in the trendiest, most modern kitchens of South Beach, the past isn't forgotten. It's updated. Honored. Re-imagined.

Modern menus take what once was rustic and make it luxurious. Ingredients are local, flavors are tropical, and presentations are bold—but the heart still beats with the rhythm of the past.

Define Your Cookery Style—Then Amplify It.
Your menu should speak in your voice.

Whether that voice echoes farm-fresh simplicity or tropical exoticism, it should be unmistakable. In South Florida, that voice often shouts: bold, tropical, fresh. Elsewhere, it might whisper rustic, soulful, or seasonal. No matter where you are, the menu must reflect the chef's ideals.

But a menu can't do it alone.

Your staff is your mouthpiece. If they don't understand your culinary philosophy, how will the guest? Educate them. Talk to them. Let them taste. When your team can explain why a dish exists, not just what's in it, that's when diners begin to truly understand your vision.

Your ideals shouldn't just be printed—
they should be communicated, championed, and
lived by everyone on the floor.

From Plating to Philosophy: Where It All Comes Together

Great cuisine is more than great food. It's vision. It's feeling. It's philosophy on a plate.

It's the soul of your upbringing + the clarity of your ideals + the discipline of repetition + the artistry of plating.

That's how you go from serving meals to shaping memories.
Your Voice.

Your Ideals.

Turmoil abounds around you. Heat, suffocating humidity and a heart pumping work-pace is more like a summertime cardio workout in the gym than it is a day of work at your chosen profession.

Chosen is the optimal word. Most young chefs dream of being that new star on the TV horizon-where all of America knows your name - but it means putting your mind and body through a rigorous work out every day.

Becoming that celebrated chef takes people listening. Approving and then buying into your ideals. In advance of molding and shaping your own Culinary voice, the uneasiness that you feel because you do not have your own voice is painful. It will only be built after years of day to day experiences.

When you begin to shape your own culinary voice, listen for advice from others. Identity creation will follow you through the rest of your cooking years.

Ask a mentor what they have taught others and then think of ways in which you might follow their conduct. Take relevant advice from everyone, shape it using your own manners structuring a renewed voice. Listen to your customers, because "if you only cook what you like to eat, you might be the only one left in your place eating", say chefs I have interviewed for this book. This will help shape your own localized cookery style. The manner in which you get to your objective might change, yet your ideals should remain constant.

Time and time again, I have changed my style according to the position I held. Every new position you take will query your culinary style. Some people want your voice to be bold and new, others want it to conform to their perceived style.

Speak with Your Voice, Lead with Your Ideals

In every kitchen I enter, I choose to lead boldly. I look for what's new, what's different, and what's possible. I experiment. I learn. I evolve. Then I raise the standard.

Once you discover your culinary voice—your ideal—you must speak it. Share it. Repeat it. Make sure your team hears it not once, but often, and understands not just what you're doing, but why.

True leadership is rooted in clarity, repetition, and trust.

Teach with Precision, Lead with Purpose.

When you teach, ask if your team understands. Then ask them to explain it back. Listen carefully. Clarify where needed. Only then do you move forward. Step by step, you build alignment.

When your culinary style starts delivering results—when guests respond, when the flow improves, when the food sings—get management on board. Make them part of the vision. Invite your staff's feedback, too. Understand what your guests are craving and how your team sees the process. Build your culinary framework around them, not just yourself.

Remember: great chefs don't demand loyalty. They earn buy-in.

Don't Just Train—Inspire.

Every kitchen has different expectations. Every region has different diners. Your ideals should be shaped by common sense and guided by the guests you want to serve. When your staff believes in your direction, they'll mentor others, share your vision with guests, and help the entire operation thrive.

I've always used real-world reinforcement. In training sessions, I role-play with my staff. Ask questions. Reward answers. If they explain the menu clearly and confidently—boom, they earn a dollar. It's fun, memorable, and effective. When they realize that better communication leads to bigger tips and better guest experiences, everyone wins.

Find Your Voice and Wear It Proudly.

The best chefs don't just cook—they communicate. They make their culinary philosophy part of the daily work flow. Everything reflects it: the mise en place, the plating, the training, the tone of the kitchen.

Look at chefs like Charlie Trotter. Even when he left his kitchen for culinary events, his restaurant never missed a beat. Why? Because his staff didn't just follow a manual—they lived his ideals. That's the power of consistent, unwavering leadership.

So be bold. Put your ideals in writing. Share them in staff

memos. Define your vocabulary and make it the language of your kitchen. When your team understands your values, they become ambassadors for your brand.

Put Your Passion in Print.

If you want others to truly understand your philosophy, put it into words. Reflect on what matters to you and why. Listen to your inner voice—the one that urges you to do better, to stay clean, to stay true. That voice is your compass. It exists for the same reason health codes exist: to protect people and build trust.

Read other chefs' books. Pay attention to how they express their values. How do they make their ideas stick? What do they highlight? Which details matter most? The more styles you explore, the stronger your own writing will become.

Compare their ideas to yours. Tell your team how your ideals align or differ. Show them how those ideals are reflected in the dishes they serve. Let them carry your message table side.

Make Your Message Feel-able.

Paint pictures with your words. Let your passion come through in every description. When someone reads your writing, they should feel it. Don't just explain a recipe—tell a story.

Say something like:

"This mango's hue looks like it was painted by a Monet-level artist."

That's what connects people. Your words create moments of imagination and emotion. They set you apart—not just as a cook, but as a communicator.

Write Recipes That Live.

As you write, include personal discoveries and creative impulses. Keep it real and accessible. Speak directly to the reader's level. Make it easy to follow and easy to replicate.

The best recipes aren't just instructions—they're journeys. Describe the evolution of the dish. Tell how a mistake led to a breakthrough. Explain why this ingredient matters. Build anticipation in your introduction. Give readers a reason to keep reading.

Then walk them through, step by step, as if you're right there beside them. Show them why this process works and how it fits into your broader culinary belief system.

Conclusion: Lead with Heart, Share with Clarity

Leadership in the kitchen isn't about ego—it's about purpose. Your voice matters. Your ideals matter. Whether you're speaking to your team, your guests, or your readers, what you say should reflect what you believe.

Speak boldly. Teach clearly. Lead with consistency. Write like someone is standing in your kitchen, learning from your every word.

That's how you build something that lasts.
Your Culinary Collections...
Your Recipes.
You are sharing your passion.

Write Like You Cook:

Recipes with Soul and Voice. Writing a recipe isn't just instruction—it's storytelling. It's a reflection of who you are as a chef, your ideals, and your passion for ingredients. Whether you're crafting a simple vinaigrette or a complex braised dish, your culinary voice should be unmistakable. It should come through in every word, every choice, and every flavor.

Start With Passion.

The best recipes don't begin with a list of ingredients—they begin with passion. What do you love about this dish? Why does it matter to you? What ingredient excites you the most?

The heart of a recipe is its story. That's what pulls the reader in. Speak honestly and clearly about your connection to the dish, the ingredients, or the memories it holds. A short, vivid preamble can instantly connect you with the reader.

"I remember the first time I tasted heirloom tomatoes still warm from the sun. That experience changed how I understood acidity, sweetness, and balance—and it's why this salad exists."

Your recipe should show your passion,
not just talk about it.

Use Your Culinary Voice.
Recipe writing is deeply personal. Your voice—shaped by your experiences in the kitchen, your mentors, your mistakes—is your signature. Make your voice come through in the instructions. Let your enthusiasm for technique, ingredient quality, and flavor shine in the way you describe even simple actions.

Don't just say "sauté the onions." Say:
"Sauté the onions until they reach that point just before they start to brown—soft, golden, and fragrant enough to stop someone walking past the kitchen." Give life to the actions. Paint pictures. Use vivid verbs and sensory language.

Keep It Clear, Not Complicated.
While your voice should be colorful, your instructions should be clear. Your audience may not have access to restaurant-grade equipment or years of culinary training. Great recipe writing bridges that gap without dumbing anything down.

Break down techniques into steps. Define any terms that aren't beginner-friendly. Anticipate where confusion might happen, and get ahead of it with explanation. If you're writing for advanced cooks, go deeper—but always guide. Show your reader what to look for, feel, smell, and taste. That's how you build trust and success.

Flavor Is the Destination.

Above all else, the recipe must taste great. Technique matters. Storytelling matters. But if the dish doesn't sing, none of it sticks.

So describe your flavors. Be bold and exact.

"This sauce leans into the natural sweetness of roasted garlic, layered with a citrus-bright finish from Meyer lemon zest and a final hit of heat that lingers just enough to make you want another bite."

Tell them why it works. Tell them how it should feel in the mouth. And if the flavor balance depends on a step or a subtlety—point it out.

Your Recipe Is a Gift.

Every recipe you write is a chance to share a piece of yourself. That's what chefs do every day—with their staff, with their guests, with their plates. Recipe writing is simply another medium for that same generosity.

Use your words to transfer confidence. If you write with energy, your reader will cook with energy. If you write with clarity, they'll cook with clarity.

If you show love for your ingredients, they'll taste that love in the finished dish.

Passion is contagious.
So is precision.
A great recipe blends both.

A Few Writing Techniques to Keep in Mind.

Open strong. Start with a personal anecdote or insight that frames the recipe. Describe with detail. Let readers see, smell, and feel each step. Be honest about difficulty. If something takes practice, say so—and encourage them. Use relate-able comparisons. ("Sauté until the leeks are the color of dry straw.") Keep it fun. A little personality goes a long way in guiding the reader through the process.

Final Thought: Cook Like an Artist, Write Like a Mentor

Writing recipes isn't just about sharing food—it's about passing on a way of thinking, a creative spirit, a dedication to detail. And yes, a bit of soul.

Whether it's the mango that looks like Monet painted it, or the fresh snap of a local green bean, help your readers feel what you feel. Show them why this matters. Show them why food, to you, isn't a job—it's a mission.

Chapter Four:

~Flavors~

Draw out and Evolve the Flavor of a Single or a Trove of Innumerable Ingredients.

What Would You Like to Express?

Creative freedom or conformity to standards—that's the dividing line. That's what defines us as chefs.

In the 1970s, French Classical tradition was gospel. If you weren't following Escoffier, you weren't cooking "correctly." Across South Florida, that meant menus filled with heavy sauces, imported seafood, and a devotion to European formality. Local flavors—mango, papaya, plantain, conch—were overlooked, dismissed as "too rustic" for serious cuisine.

But this era of imitation couldn't last forever. By the 1980s and 90s, the tides shifted. Chefs began breaking away from Old World orthodoxy and looking instead to their own backyard. The result was a turning point: South Florida stopped being a follower and started becoming a leader. The boldness of individuality collided with the region's cultural mix, and suddenly French sauces met Caribbean heat, Latin zest, and tropical sweetness.

This was more than a style change—it was a revolution. South Florida's kitchens began speaking with their own voice, one that echoed its geography, its immigrant communities, and its sun-soaked abundance. What had once been a culinary backwater became a crucible of innovation, setting the stage for the food scene that now defines the region.

And it's not just the professionals. The ripple effect of this shift reaches into every kitchen. Every home cook, every parent flipping through a cookbook, is searching for creative permission—a fresh spin on a familiar dish, a theme that excites, a recipe that whispers: go ahead, make it yours.

For me, cookbooks aren't rulebooks. They're launchpads. Starters. Blueprints that give you just enough structure to begin—and then invite you to veer off halfway through prep, guided by taste, memory, or instinct. That's the beauty of expression in the kitchen: controlled chaos, shaped not by rigid technique but by curiosity and confidence.

This democratization of creativity—chefs finding their own voice, home cooks refusing to color inside the lines—completes the picture of a true turning point. It's the moment when food stopped being about conformity and started being about identity. And nowhere has that identity shone brighter than in South Florida, where individuality and cultural mix have become the flavor profile of an entire region.

Framing the Essence:
I'm currently focused on the user's input, particularly the title. It seems like the core theme is freedom and creativity, as suggested by "South Florida: A Playground of Freedom". I'm analyzing how these concepts might be embodied in the

user's input and how best to articulate them.

Expanding on the Theme:

I've been examining the user's input, specifically how the "playground of freedom" theme translates into the food scene. The phrases like "culinary rules bend" and "traditions mix" immediately signal the core of the user's focus: a melting pot of culinary innovation where creativity flourishes. I'm exploring how to weave that into a compelling response.

Refining the Narrative:

I'm now zeroing in on the intersection of cultural influences and culinary innovation in South Florida. The geographical and cultural melting pot paints a vibrant picture. I'm focusing on weaving these diverse elements together, highlighting the freedom from traditional culinary constraints.

Crafting a Compelling Response:

I'm now focusing on integrating the various influencing factors to the user's focus on freedom in South Florida's food scene. I'm aiming to craft a compelling response that validates and expands on the initial sentiment, tying in the rich cultural blend, the bountiful local ingredients, and the overall vibrant culinary atmosphere. I'm working to give it a unique voice.

Unpacking the Scene:

I'm now diving into the user's focus on South Florida's food scene as a "playground." I'm looking at how the various cultural influences, from Cuba to Haiti to the Jewish diaspora, have shaped the culinary landscape. I'm exploring the nuances of these influences, aiming to paint a vibrant picture of this culinary melting pot.

Reflecting the Culinary Tapestry:

I'm now focusing on the vibrant cultural blend within South Florida's food scene. This is where Latin American traditions, Caribbean influences, and other diverse culinary practices intermingle. I'm aiming to showcase this melting pot in a dynamic, flavorful response.

The Melting Pot Perfected:

It's not just a mix, it's a true fusion. A dash of Haitian spice in a traditionally Jewish dish, a Peruvian ceviche technique applied to local Florida snapper, the comforting warmth of Southern soul food served alongside a meticulously crafted Cuban cortadito. This is where "authenticity" isn't about rigid adherence to one tradition, but the honest expression of many.

A Pantry of Abundance:

That freedom is fueled by the ingredients themselves. Chefs have the bounty of the Atlantic at their doorstep and a tropical climate that yields exotic fruits and produce year-round. The menu is written by the sea and the sun.

A Culture of Reinvention:

South Florida has always been a place for new beginnings. That spirit attracts people—chefs, artists, entrepreneurs—who aren't afraid to break the mold and create something entirely new. The result is a dining scene that is constantly surprising, challenging, and delighting its audience.

The Great Collision: Precision Meets Passion:

The Transplant Energy: Chefs arrive from New York, Chicago, or L.A. carrying a toolkit of rigorous, often European-based techniques. They understand discipline, logistics, and the relentless pursuit of perfection required to survive in those hyper-competitive markets. They bring the structure.

The Southern Heat: They land in a place pulsating with a different rhythm. The air is thick with the aromas of sofrito and the sounds of Spanish, Creole, and Portuguese. The culinary landscape is shaped by generations of instinctual, tradition-rich cooking from Cuba, Colombia, Peru, Haiti, and beyond. This is the spontaneity and the soul.

The magic happens when that northern precision is applied to the untamed, vibrant flavors of the south. A meticulously executed French technique might be used to elevate a humble mofongo. A Japanese approach to sourcing and slicing fish is applied to local wahoo or hogfish, served with a passionfruit leche de tigre. It's a dialogue between worlds on a single plate.

Designing Experiences, Not Just Dinners

Your point about designing experiences is crucial. In South Florida, the "vibe" is an essential ingredient.

A meal isn't just consumed; it's an event. The setting—whether it's a stunning waterfront view, a lush hidden courtyard, or a room throbbing with a curated DJ set—is as much a part of the menu as the food itself. This is where chefs become producers. They understand that their audience, a mix of savvy locals and international visitors, craves a full sensory immersion. They are building a narrative from the moment a guest walks in, blending high-concept cuisine with an atmosphere that feels effortlessly glamorous and alive.

This is why South Florida's food scene feels so singular right now. It has the technical brilliance and ambition of a global capital, but it's fueled by a local culture so rich and dynamic that it forces everyone—even the most established chefs—to innovate, adapt, and create something undeniably new. It's bold, it's loud, and it is entirely its own.

Bold Flavors, Bold Identity.
As chefs, our identity is defined by what we put on the plate. Bold flavors aren't just about heat or intensity—they're about confidence. They tell your guests: this is who I am, and this is what I believe food should be.

That's culinary freedom. That's what I chase in every dish I make. And that's what I hope every cook—home or professional—feels empowered to do: express themselves through food, with no apologies.

Coupling of Flavors

Getting flavors to meld around each other is how I experiment with new recipes.

Flavor bonding is the art of pairing contrasting yet complementary tastes—like acid with fat or sweet with savory—to create a balanced and harmonious dish. Symmetry in this context refers to the scientific process, often using emulsifiers, that physically and chemically binds these ingredients together into a stable, unified structure.

Flavor Bonding: The Art of Harmonious Contrast

At its heart, flavor bonding is about creating a taste experience that is greater than the sum of its parts. It works on the principle that contrasting elements can accentuate and elevate one another. Think of it like a musical chord; individual notes are fine, but when played together in harmony, they create a much richer sound.

Coulis-grette is a perfect example.

The Sweet: The base is the sweet, tropical flavor of the mango puree. The Acid: Vinegar is added not to make it sour, but to "sharpen" the mango's natural brightness, cutting through the sweetness so it doesn't taste flat.

The Fat: Olive oil rounds out the sharp edges of the vinegar and adds a rich, velvety mouthfeel, making the sauce cling to the food.

Without this deliberate bonding, the individual flavors would clash or fall flat. With it, you achieve a balanced profile where each component makes the others better.

The Science of Symmetry: Emulsions and Binders.

While flavor bonding is the "why," emulsification is often the scientific "how." An emulsion is a mixture of two liquids that normally don't mix, like oil and water. The key to holding them together is an emulsifier—an ingredient that has a unique molecular structure, with one end attracted to water and the other attracted to oil.

This is the science behind classics like mayonnaise. The lecithin in egg yolks acts as a powerful emulsifier, grabbing onto both the oil and the vinegar (or lemon juice) and forcing them to bond into a creamy, stable sauce. The egg yolk is the bridge that creates the symmetry between otherwise incompatible ingredients.

Modern Applications and Evolution

As you noted, the art of binding evolves with guest preferences and culinary innovation. The rise of molecular gastronomy has introduced a new toolkit for chefs.

Meeting Dietary Needs: For vegan guests or those with egg allergies, traditional emulsions are off-limits. Vegetable starches (like arrowroot) or hydrocolloids (gums like xanthan gum) can be used to create stable, creamy textures without any animal products.

Creative Control: These modern binders offer incredible precision. They allow chefs to create sauces, foams, and gels with unique textures that aren't possible with traditional ingredi-

ents, pushing the boundaries of what a dish can be.
Whether using a classic egg yolk or a modern vegetable gum, the fundamental goal remains the same: to create a pleasing symmetry that bonds distinct flavors into a single, delicious vision.

Classics and Chemistry:
Bonding isn't just modern—it's classical. It's what makes lamb beg for rosemary, or apple tartin feel naked without its caramel. These combinations transcend trend—they're structural. They're bonded by centuries of tradition and taste memory.

Take demi-glace. My twist? Tamarind. Its acidic, prune-like richness—famously hidden in Worcestershire—amplifies the depth of the sauce like nothing else. That's a flavor bond I rely on.

Every chef builds a mental library of these ideals:

- Basil in tomato sauce — non-negotiable.
- Meringue with Key lime pie — expected and harmonious.
- Grated cheese on grilled fish — a mismatch of ideals.

Bonding, in essence, is about integrity. It's about knowing which flavors naturally belong together and which ones clash.

Bonding is the chemistry, but balance is the poetry. It's the skill that separates a well-executed recipe from a truly memorable dish.

That ability to “taste it in your head” is the mark of an experienced chef. It’s an internal, intuitive database built from years of tasting, experimenting, and understanding the very personality of each ingredient. You can mentally simulate the reaction, predicting how the assertive acidity of a passionfruit will interact with the earthy bitterness of greens, or how a specific spice will bloom when toasted in oil.

The Yin and Yang on the Plate:
The Yin and Yang philosophy is the perfect metaphor for this culinary balancing act. It’s about creating a dynamic harmony where opposing forces don’t cancel each other out, but rather complete and elevate one another.

Yin represents the rich, earthy, fatty, and cooling elements. The grounding forces of a dish. Yang represents the bright, acidic, spicy, and sharp elements. The forces that excite and awaken the palate.

A dish with too much Yin is heavy, monotonous, and cloying. A dish with too much Yang is aggressive, sharp, and overwhelming. The art is in the equilibrium.

A Key Largo Example
Right now, looking out at the water as evening approaches, I can taste a perfectly balanced dish in my head. Let’s start with the Yin: a beautiful, pan-seared fillet of local Hogfish. It’s rich, with a delicate, almost sweet nuttiness. On its own, it’s

pleasant but one-dimensional. It needs its counterpart.
Now, we introduce the Yang to achieve balance:
Acid: A light sauce made from Key lime juice to cut through the richness of the fish.

Sweetness: A finely diced salsa of ripe mango and sweet bell pepper to complement the fish's natural sweetness without overpowering it.

Heat: A micro-mince of scotch bonnet pepper in that salsa, just enough to leave a whisper of warmth on the back of the palate.

Aromatics & Bitterness: A sprinkle of fresh, sharp cilantro to provide a fresh, herbal lift.

The balance is a tightrope walk. Too much lime and you've just made ceviche. Too much mango and the dish turns into a dessert. Not enough salt, and none of these flavors will pop; they'll remain isolated components. When the balance is right, you taste the fish, the lime, the sweet, and the heat all in one harmonious bite. The components no longer fight; they dance.

This is the daily challenge and the ultimate reward—creating that perfect, fleeting moment of symmetry on the palate.

I was taught:
"The difference between a chef and a cook is in the seasoning." That means knowing your ingredients well enough to lift

their natural flavor—not bury it.

Seasoning isn't about overpowering. It's about nudging a dish into brilliance. Not stealing the spotlight from the ingredient—but putting a soft, flattering light on it.

""Like Deserves Like" – Smart Flavor Pairing.

Balance doesn't always come from contrast. Sometimes, it comes from alignment—pairing flavors that echo and amplify one another, creating depth through harmony rather than tension.

Take grilled tuna and soy sauce as an example. On the grill, tuna develops a smoky, almost steak-like quality. Pair it with a naturally brewed soy that's been aged in charred oak barrels, and suddenly the flavors resonate. The oak from the fire and the oak from the barrel are speaking the same language, reinforcing each other in layers.

That's the essence of "like deserves like." It's a reminder that balance in cooking isn't only about opposites attracting—it's also about finding common threads and weaving them tighter. When done thoughtfully, this approach creates flavors that feel inevitable, as if they always belonged together.

Same goes for roasting. A beef roast sits atop a bed of mirepoix. As the meat roasts, juices drip, vegetables caramelize, and flavors mingle. Later, you deglazed that pan, lift those flavors into your demi-glace, and suddenly—every element enhances the next. The sauce doesn't compete with the meat—it completes it.

True vs. Borrowed Flavors:

The true flavor of food lives in its raw state. A tomato sliced open, a peach bitten into, a leaf torn from the stem. That's the baseline—the unedited voice of the ingredient.

Cooking bends that truth. Heat softens and sweetens. Acid brightens. Fat carries. Salt amplifies. Char adds depth, smoke adds memory. Each one a borrowed flavor layered on top of the original.

What we love in a dish is rarely the naked truth—it's the interplay. The honesty of what the food is, plus the masks we give it. Rawness and transformation, held in balance.

Ceviche, for example, borrows the sharp transformation of lime juice to "cook" raw fish. Without the lime, it's just sushi. Barbecue without smoke? It loses its soul. Cooking, at its heart, is controlled transformation—building flavor upon flavor without losing sight of where it started.

Conclusion: The Chef's Flavor Code

Flavor isn't accidental. It's a language. A philosophy. A system of belief every serious chef holds close.

- Bonding creates structure.
- Symmetry creates harmony.
- Seasoning creates integrity.
- Respect for original flavor preserves the soul.

Cooking is where science and instinct meet. And for those of us who live this life, it's not just about what tastes good—it's about what feels right.

The Power of Borrowed Flavor and the Evolution of Restraint

Flavors are everything. Without them, cuisine wouldn't exist—at least not in the way we know it. Raw food is fuel. Cooked food, flavored food, becomes culture.

As proteins cook, they release moisture—those juices often find their way into the pan, where they caramelize from the heat breaking down the meat's fibers. This moment is more than science—it's opportunity. That flavor-laden fond left behind becomes the foundation for sauce. Once deglazed, it transforms into something greater than the sum of its parts. This is borrowed flavor—the silent signature of the cooking process, lending its character to the final dish.

Borrowed Flavor: The Quiet Backbone of Great Cooking

Borrowed flavors don't only come from the pan. They arrive in the form of marinades, rubs, or seasoning blends that may burn off during cooking but leave behind undeniable traces. They're ghosts of flavor—enhancers without overwhelming the dish.

Take rosemary. Fresh, it's potent. Mishandled, it's overpowering. But toast it lightly in a scorching pan, and it releases its essential oils. You lose the raw, pungent green. What's left behind is toasted pine, subtle perfume, and a caramelized aromatic that enhances, rather than hijacks, a lamb roast. That's the art: flavor that supports, not steals.

The same goes for onions. Slowly caramelizing them until golden transforms sharpness into sweetness. In onion soup, this transformation is essential. The soup doesn't just taste like onions—it tastes like onions that have become something else. That's borrowed flavor, developed with time, heat, and care.

From Loud to Layered: A Shift in Culinary Thinking:

In the heyday of New World Cuisine—South Florida circa 1995—it was all about impact. Chefs competed to blast your taste buds with boldness. Dishes were built to jolt, not whisper. Acidity, spice, sweetness, umami—every bite was a fireworks show.

And while that era was exciting, we've since learned something valuable: restraint takes more skill than force. To know when to hold back. To let quiet flavors breathe. To layer instead of stack.

Today's best cooking isn't about who can shout the loudest—it's about who can keep you leaning in. Subtlety, balance, patience: these are the marks of maturity in the kitchen. The shift is less from bland to bold, and more from loud to layered.

Modern Cookery:

Modern cookery—especially in refined kitchens across South Florida—has shifted from overwhelming to enhancing. No longer about drowning mediocre ingredients under heavy reductions or explosive sauces. The best chefs now start with quality and trust it. They know when to season lightly, when to leave space, when to step back and let the food speak.

It's a quieter confidence: enhancing instead of masking, revealing instead of disguising. The ingredient holds the spotlight, and technique plays the supporting role.

Borrowed flavors still have a place, but they work in harmony. They don't dominate; they elevate. They don't mask; they amplify.

Brazen Flavor with Purpose

Bold flavors still matter—but now they're built with intention. Chefs craft dishes with willful intensity, not reckless spice. It's the difference between a slap and a symphony. You still get the punch—but it's part of a bigger story, not the whole show. This kind of cooking is personal. It shows maturity. It's proof that a chef has evolved—not just in technique, but in taste. Knowing what to leave out is just as important as knowing what to put in.

Conclusion: Let Flavor Work, Not Shout

The best flavors don't scream. They linger, support, and echo through every element of the dish.

Borrowed flavors are the foundation of great cooking. But like any good foundation, they're not meant to be the focus. Let them be the reason your food tastes complete, not crowded.

Flavor Borrowing or Blasting your Tastebuds

Sweetness, Subtlety, and the Communion of Flavor

As Miami chefs embraced fresher, higher-quality ingredients, the need to shock the palate faded. No longer did we need to drown seafood in sauce or blast the guest's taste buds into unconsciousness to impress. Today, true flavor—clean, bold, balanced—stands on its own.

Real Deliciousness: Sweetness vs. Subtlety

There's no denying it—Americans gravitate toward sweetness. Just check the ingredient labels in your pantry: corn syrup, malto-dextrin, glycerol—sweetness is built into nearly everything. That said, sweetness isn't universal, and it doesn't belong everywhere. But used well, it connects. It comforts. It delivers.

Natural sweetness—like that of a ripe tomato or freshly picked green bean—shouldn't be overpowering. It should be subtle, expected, and balanced. I often bring this principle into play by pairing slightly sweet elements, like mango salsa, with savory dishes like Caribbean-spiced grouper. The balance—Yin to Yang—is what creates satisfaction on the plate. Not intensity. Not excess. Just harmony.

Think of a dish with one sweet, one savory, and one neutral element. That triangle of taste is how we, as chefs, build a pleasurable experience—not just a meal.

The Complexity Within Simplicity.
The culinary philosophy that resonates most with me is this: find the intricate within the simple. That's where the soul of cuisine lives.

A freshly grilled, herb-roasted Yellowtail snapper with nothing more than sea salt and rosemary can be just as memorable as a multi-component fine-dining plate. Simplicity—when executed with skill—is profound.

Take mangoes. Their flavor spectrum is wildly complex—citrus, guava, pine, apple, even carrot-like notes—but they still deliver one unifying message: mango. The layers are subtle, and recognizing them is like tasting through a flight of Cabernet Sauvignons. The nuances of terroir, ripeness, and growing conditions echo in every bite. That's why we love wine—and it's why we should love fruit with the same reverence.

Flavor Is a Calling—and a Niche.
As chefs, our personal flavor philosophies define our food—and often our careers. Some call it a niche, others a calling. I call it common sense. Cooking what's fresh, what's local, what's part of your regional food culture—that's not a restriction. That's creative liberation.

In South Florida, I gravitate naturally toward "Caribb-ican" cuisine. The tropical ingredients, the Caribbean influence, the agricultural abundance of Florida—it all aligns. I don't need to invent exotic flavors. They're already here.

A Softer Touch: The South Florida Flavor Shift.

Caribbean cuisine is known for boldness and heat. But South Florida offers a gentler take—bright, fresh, and modern. Where once we scorched the senses, now we guide them. This shift reflects the times. Diners crave flavor, but they want it with finesse. A light mango-lime vinaigrette instead of a heavy glaze. A grilled pineapple relish instead of butter-drenched sauces. The heat is still there—but it's thoughtful. We season with care in a social media world where every plate tells a story before the first bite.

The Economics of Simplicity.

Florida, being one of the top agricultural states, gives chefs direct access to exceptional produce. In Caribbean food traditions, vegetables and starches dominate—not because of trend, but out of necessity. Proteins cost more, so generations learned to make the most of garden harvests.

That necessity evolved into a defining feature of Caribbean cooking: produce-forward, flavor-rich, budget-conscious. Today, it's not just practical—it's culinary heritage. It's sustainable. It's smart.

And sauces? They're not afterthoughts—they're economic strategy. A good sauce can make a modest portion of protein feel indulgent. A cream-finished demi-glace, like the one on steak Diane, gives richness and satiety without relying on large protein portions. That's not just flavor—it's business sense.

Communion of Ingredients: Where Flavor Becomes Philosophy.

Natural ingredients play well together. When paired thoughtfully, they become more than the sum of their parts. Sea salt and seafood. Rosemary and roasted lamb. Mango and lime. Soy sauce and grilled tuna. These combinations feel right—because they are.

"Like deserves like" isn't just a culinary truth—
it's a flavor philosophy.

A great dish creates a commune—a flavor ecosystem where everything complements, nothing competes. The "Asian Trinity" of powdered ginger, wasabi, and soy sauce is a perfect example. The heat, tang, and salt combine in a seamless balance of fire and finesse. Even the classic fruit salsa shows how nature offers harmony: spicy, sweet, fresh, acidic. It's bright. It's natural. It's health-forward. And it's pure South Florida.

Some Flavor Combinations Are Just Right.

At the end of the day, the best dishes don't try too hard. They feel inevitable. Like they've always existed.

- Grilled fish crusted in sea salt and rosemary.
- Steak Diane balanced with cream.
- A tomato-onion salsa with citrus zest folded in at the last second.
- A mango coulis matched with savory blackened seafood.

That's the communion of ingredients. That's how flavor becomes memory. And that's the chef's job: to guide, not dominate. To balance, not bombard. To express, not impose.

The Value in the Quintessential: Garnishing as the Mark of a Chef. Does value in the culinary world equate to complexity in garnishing?

Adding a side dish to a protein is easy. But integrating a garnish—one with a specific counterbalance that elevates the entire preparation—is a task requiring refined skill and perseverance. Chefs wear this challenge like a talisman, just as surely as they wear their neckerchiefs.

During economic downturns, many restaurants equate value with plate volume: large portions meant to satisfy hunger and justify the price. In contrast, fine dining establishments focus on the art of presentation. Guests eat with their eyes first, and both approaches appeal to different dining mentalities. One guest might feel satisfied seeing a heaping plate. Another may take joy in the finesse of a minimal yet elegant composition. Both find value because their expectations are met—or even exceeded.

Personally, I believe in the latter approach. True value lies in artistic presentation. A dish so beautiful that a diner hesitates to eat without snapping a photo first—that is the real culinary achievement. Walk into any metropolitan fine dining restaurant and you'll see this trend. Most chefs I've interviewed agree: no matter how much food is on the plate, if it looks fantastic, it offers the best value.

As one of my mentors at the Culinary Institute said, "It's all in the garnishment." A refined, minimal garnish brings dimension, balance, and distinction to a plate. The simplicity of economy becomes grandeur through thoughtful execution. A beautiful plate isn't complex in volume—but in vision.

Culinary Aesthetics: If It Tastes Delicious, Does It Give Joy?
What makes a chef grand? Is it the deliciousness of their food—or the character of the person behind the plate?

In many cases, it's the latter.

Consider Chef Charlie Trotter's legendary Chicago restaurant. His culinary philosophy shaped every aspect of the operation. His media-celebrated success wasn't accidental. It was grounded in a relentless attention to detail. Charlie didn't just create great recipes—he fostered a culture where excellence was non-negotiable. From dishwasher to server, every team member knew that pleasing the guest was the top priority.

No matter how many accolades a dish receives, if the guest isn't happy—if the food doesn't feel right to them—then it's not right. Taste is relative. Meeting and exceeding the guest's expectations is the mark of a true chef.

Deliciousness, too, is subjective. We can't guess someone's palate by looking at them. Some cultures prefer their meats fully cooked; others love rare preparations. If a guest wants their duck breast or tuna loin well done—and it gives them joy—then that is the right way for them. A chef's task is not to impose tradition, but to deliver satisfaction.

Taste Great
And does
it give pleasure?

The Value in the Quintessential: Garnishing as the Mark of a Chef. Does value in the culinary world equate to complexity in garnishing?

Adding a side dish to a protein is easy. But integrating a garnish—one with a specific counterbalance that elevates the entire preparation—is a task requiring refined skill and perseverance. Chefs wear this challenge like a talisman, just as surely as they wear their neckerchiefs.

Fusion, Form, and the New Culinary Common Sense:
The synthesis of our many diverse cookery styles can be daunting—yet it remains deeply rewarding for the palate. Take, for example, the way a Spanish flair for starch can harmonize perfectly with the fire of an equatorial Haitian or Jamaican sauce. This interplay of heat and comfort is what makes fusion cuisine so exhilarating.

For decades, formal dining has embraced the visual drama of intimate portions on oversized plates—aesthetic elegance that also happens to benefit the bottom line. Our foundation in French culinary training has evolved from the minimalism of nouvelle cuisine, where white space dominated the plate, into a modern era of architecturally expressive presentations.

The French tradition fuels our passion for fanciful, artistic expression, even while its classical rules once demanded strict uniformity. Variety was rarely a consideration in the old brigade kitchens. Today, however, we've broken those chains. Our plating is free-form, our cooking styles border on the experimental. In the kitchens of South Florida, this "mad scientist" approach isn't just accepted—it's celebrated.

The rigid foodways of pre-colonial France are now as passé as last year's New Year's resolutions. Chefs in South Florida thrive on being at the forefront of the new. It's not just about cooking—it's about creativity, reinvention, and momentum. Being on the cusp of a culinary evolution is our standard.

Creativity & Common Sense: The Power of No-Brainers

At its core, being a chef is about creativity. But creativity must always be balanced with common sense—especially when it comes to profitability. This is where the concept of the no-brainer comes in. These are dishes that deliver both ingenuity and dependable profit margins.

As chefs, we push ourselves to innovate, to chase trends and define the next wave of dining. Yet in the process, we sometimes overlook the simple, consistent work that keeps the lights on. Every menu needs its no-brainers: the dishes everyone loves, that always sell, that always earn.

Think about pizza. It's the ultimate no-brainer. But when Wolfgang Puck turned pizza into a gourmet concept, he created something more—he fused profitability with trend setting. That's the chef's sweet spot: innovation that pays.

Chef Michael Bloise found his own version of this balance at his latest concept, The Noodle Bar. There, he crafts gourmet noodle dishes served in bowls and small plates—an Asian-influenced cuisine offered at accessible, urban-friendly prices. Guests can explore new flavors without sticker shock, and the restaurant thrives.

What's more, the open-kitchen design allows Chef Michael to connect with diners firsthand. Rather than being hidden behind drywall and swinging doors, he's at the heart of the action—communing with guests and experiencing their satisfaction in real time.

Even the design was a no-brainer: one efficient, exhibition-style kitchen powering the entire restaurant. This simplicity lets the chef engage with the dining room, orchestrate the experience, and maintain profitability—all without sacrificing his creative drive.

Conclusion: The Modern Culinary Mindset.
Today's chef must be both artist and entrepreneur. We embrace fusion and experimentation while grounding our operations in smart, profitable choices. Whether it's through beautifully composed plates or crowd-pleasing menu staples, our goal remains the same: create joy, connect with guests, and push the boundaries—one no-brainer at a time.

Free-forming your ideals...

Lose the Boundaries and Molds

Breaking the Mold: South Florida's Culinary Rebellion

In South Florida, boundaries exist only to be broken.

As discussed earlier, without culinary tradition, chefs would be reinventing every dish from scratch every time they stepped behind a sauté pan. That's where the concept of the mold comes in—a foundation, not a prison. A mold exists to be broken. And nothing better illustrates the energy behind the stainless-steel bulkheads of South Florida kitchens.

Boundaries and molds give a chef a place to begin, a direction from which to depart. They help shape a unique culinary thesis. In the early days of New World Cuisine, these molds served as launching pads for an entirely new cookery heritage. Local farmers, proud of their tropical bounty, partnered with South Florida chefs, offering excess harvests as creative fuel. My friends in the Rare Fruit Council often gave me their surplus mangoes, starfruit, and papayas—delivered not just as ingredients but as inspiration.

With these gifts came creative freedom. Freed from cost constraints, we experimented with abandon. The result? Innovation with no fear, recipes with no road map. It was a no-brainer.

We broke the mold every single day.

I remember marinating thin-sliced swamp cabbage in citrus juice and pairing it with a mosaic of tropical fruits—creating a salad as refreshing as it was bold. This wasn't just a new dish; it was an entirely new language of flavor. And it happened because we weren't afraid to push boundaries. During the golden era of New World Cuisine (circa 1992–2002), we carried the torch for a new kind of valor: culinary nascence.

To be bold, to be new, to be untested—that was the new standard.

It takes both pride and bravery to become a culinary mad scientist. But that's what we were: chefs stretching the known universe of food, experimenting daily to redefine the rules of dining.

An Element of Tryst: The Intimacy of the Plate

A tryst—a secret meeting of lovers. In the kitchen, a tryst becomes something more: the passionate exchange between chef and guest, communicated through flavor, texture, and scent.

Today's South Florida chef plays a role unrecognizable just two decades ago. He's a community leader, an artist, and a rebel—all at once. The rebel chef expresses his individuality through the dishes he presents. His menus defy expectation. His ingredients challenge assumptions. His guests respond not only with admiration but affection. Perhaps that's the real love affair—the guest falling for the chef's ability to surprise, delight, and push boundaries with every bite.

There's romance in this defiance. Perhaps it's in the chef's wizardry, in the magic that unfolds with each plate. Or maybe it's in the way he leads his tight brigade of kitchen warriors, earning respect not just from diners, but from the community as a whole.

Whatever the reason, there's an undeniable tryst between chefs and South Florida itself. Because sometimes—whether or not tradition demands it—it just feels good to step outside the boundaries.

A Tryst with Tradition: Creativity vs. Conformity in Modern Cuisine.

Describing South Florida's culinary spirit as a tryst may seem unconventional—but it's fitting. This is no ordinary relationship between chef and cuisine. It's intimate. Subtle. Rebellious. At times, even clandestine.

In truth, New American regional cookery—especially in South Florida—flirts along the edges of classical French tradition with what can only be described as riotous apathy. We've inherited the structure, the method, and the precision of classical French cuisine. But we don't live within it—we dance around it, reinterpret it, and, when necessary, reject it entirely.

Yes, French technique still forms the backbone of many great American kitchens. But where today's regional cuisine truly thrives is at the fringes—where boundaries are blurred and rules are re-imagined. This is where innovation lives.

True creativity requires us to hold the rules loosely. It is not enough to be different for difference's sake. Breaking from tradition must serve a greater purpose than attracting attention or boosting profits. A dish should evolve not because the market demands it, but because the chef's vision compels it. Innovation must make sense. It must honor both self-respect and professional integrity. To distort your culinary philosophy solely for commercial gain is not evolution—it's erosion.

This is where great chefs draw the line. Creativity should not be chaotic. It should be intentional, meaningful, and grounded in respect—for ingredients, for process, and for the diners we serve.

PART TWO:

Chapter Five:
Chefs and Foodies...
That have made Ideals a reality.

A Day in the Life of a South Florida Chef

The coastline of South Florida draws thousands of visitors every year. There's something about the rhythmic pounding of the surf that makes it a pleasure—not just to relax—but to work by the sea. This allure continues to attract chefs from around the world to our shores.

As you cruise to work in your classic red convertible, the sun hits you differently today. You realize it's Monday—the beach has finally had a moment to recover from another 24-hour weekend party. As you cross the last bridge into Miami Beach, five 40-foot Cigarette boats race north. Their spray drifts into the air, catching your face with a cool mist and snapping you out of your morning reverie. The sunlight reflects off the millionaire mansions that tower like polished glass temples—your reality begins again.

You pull up to your “Kingdom du Jour” just as two sleek silhouettes weave through a thickening crowd. South Beach is in full swing. You’re momentarily distracted by the parade of beautiful people—shapely, sun-drenched, and endlessly on display. Here, everyone is a model, and every model waits tables between auditions. Models, model-wannabes, model-chasers, and model-makers will all soon pass through your doors to taste what others travel across the globe to experience.

Inside the restaurant, you sit with the manager to review last night’s numbers. There’s already buzz about tonight’s service: another VIP has joined the reservation list. Athletes, musicians, film and television personalities—they’ve all found a playground in the palm-lined, Art Deco dreamscape of South Beach. Your restaurant has become one of their favored stops on the “Noshing Tour de Beach.”

As the Indian summer sky fades from yellow-orange to violet, the dining room fills. The night becomes your stage. South Beach is Florida’s nightlife capital, and as the languages of German, French, and Spanish float over the buzz of conversation, you begin your nightly ritual. You are Merlin, and this is your culinary magic show.

The Players Who Crafted the Cuisine

To all those who helped shape my culinary journey—thank you.

From Islands to Icons: The History of South Florida's New World Cuisine:

Caribbean Roots: The Blueprint of Flavor:

For chefs in South Florida, especially over the last two decades, the Caribbean wasn't just a neighbor—it was a mentor. Chefs from Jamaica, Cuba, and the Dominican Republic forged techniques and flavor sensibilities that were catalytic. They introduced the power of tropical ingredients—spices, citrus, tropical fruit, yams, and fresh seafood—and a cooking mentality that prized integrity and vibrancy in raw ingredients.

This was more than influence; it was the root system of what would become New World Cuisine in South Florida.

The "Mango Gang" and the Rise of Floribbean Cuisine:

By the late 1980s and early 1990s, a quartet of visionary chefs—Norman Van Aken, Douglas Rodriguez, Mark Militello, and Allen Susser—popularized a style that synthesized Caribbean brightness with fine-dining technique. Time magazine called it "Miamiamerican." Their cuisine celebrated local staples—mango, papaya, plantain, guava, key lime, yuca, and regional fish—while layering acidity, spice, and umami in radical new ways.

Van Aken, considered the founding father of New World Cuisine, wanted to "salvage the golden treasures and vibrant calypso flavors of old Key West" and fuse them with a modern sensibility and personal expression

The cuisine even earned its own name—Floribbean—characterized by bold spice tempered by tropical sweetness

A Regional Movement Takes Flight:

Miami and South Florida answered. The "Mango Gang" sparked a wave of national attention: food writers from Time, Bon Appétit, Gourmet, and Esquire descended, hyping Miami as a must-visit culinary destination of the early 1990s. "A generation of young chefs has made Florida cuisines a New World marvel worth a detour".

Local press fueled the momentum, celebrating the region as "inspired," "sex-appeal"-rich, and ready for international scrutiny.

The Rise of the "New American Riviera":

Fast forward to today, and Miami's culinary culture is experiencing another transformation: a quiet recalibration. Dubbed a "rogue wave," this rebirth isn't flashy—it's reflective. A new generation—many homegrown, others returning after national stints—are doubling down on Miami for their voices, not just their views.

Take Michael Beltran of Ariete. A Cuban-American, he avoids tourist clichés like mango salsa, instead reinterpreting Floridian ingredients—malanga, papaya leche de tigre, local snapper—through elegant, personal lenses. His ambition isn't Michelin stars—it's a legacy for the community.

This new wave finds authenticity in neighborhood narratives and ingredients, not in tourist traffic or disposable trends. It's a culinary culture confident in its identity, comfortable enough to slow down and let ingredients—rather than flash—lead the conversation.

The Full Arc: From Roots, Through Revolution, to Reinvention:
Blueprint Phase: Caribbean kitchens laid the foundation with unmasked, tropical integrity.
Revelation Phase: The "Mango Gang" engineered Floribbean cuisine—bold, branded regional fusion.
Rebirth Phase: Today's chefs anchor themselves in Miami with restraint and specificity, cultivating a sophisticated, local-first narrative.

That's a fantastic angle—you're giving Santo Domingo its overdue recognition while connecting it directly to Miami's food identity. Here's a fuller, more historical treatment in your same sharp style:

Santo Domingo: The Forgotten Mother City
Many outsiders assume Miami cuisine is simply Cuban. But look closer and you'll find another root: Santo Domingo.
The Dominican Republic's capital, one of the oldest European-founded cities in the New World, was a culinary crossroads centuries before Miami ever existed.

It was here that Spain planted its first serious colonial ambitions in the Americas. From Santo Domingo flowed cattle, sugar, citrus, rice, and wheat—alongside enslaved Africans, whose foodways merged with Indigenous Taíno traditions. The result was a layered cuisine: sofrito, plantains, beans, slow-stewed meats, tropical fruits, all carrying the fingerprints of three continents.

Dominican cooking didn't stay put. Migrants carried it north, into Puerto Rico, Cuba, and eventually Miami. With one of the Caribbean's largest populations, Santo Domingo became both incubator and exporter. Its food culture—bold, resourceful, built on fusion—laid quiet groundwork for what South Florida chefs later celebrated as "New World Cuisine."

To talk about Miami food without acknowledging Santo Domingo is to miss half the story. Cuba may have been the loudest voice, but Santo Domingo was the mother city—the place where the fusion of African, European, and Indigenous flavors first began to hum, long before Miami learned to listen.

Spain's first colonial ambitions took hold here. African, European, and Indigenous Taíno foodways collided, producing dishes that still define Dominican cooking—and quietly shaped South Florida's own palate.

Take mangú: a simple mash of boiled green plantains, served with onions, eggs, or fried cheese. In Miami, plantain mash became a versatile side, appearing on both Dominican and

Cuban tables, and later reimagined by New World chefs as a refined base for seafood or pork. Or Sancocho: a slow, hearty stew of meats, root vegetables, and tropical tubers. Its Dominican version remains a ritual dish, but its influence echoes in Miami's love for long-simmered flavors—seen in everything from Cuban ajiaco to the braised preparations on fine-dining menus.

Then there's pastelón: a layered casserole of sweet plantains, ground meat, and cheese. Its DNA is visible in Miami's embrace of sweet-savory pairings—plantains with beef, maduros tucked into sandwiches, even haute versions plated at white-tablecloth restaurants.

These dishes weren't tourist inventions. They were daily fare—hearty, practical, deeply communal. And when Dominican migrants brought them to South Florida, they carried not only flavors but a template: food that balances the rustic with the celebratory, the humble with the generous.

So while Cuba may have defined Miami's culinary accent, Santo Domingo gave it grammar. To forget that is to miss the city's mother tongue.

Modern Miami is, in many ways, Santo Domingo's sister city—connected not only by shared climate and ingredients but by flavor and spirit. Seafood, tropical fruit, starchy roots, and slow-cooked meats define both places. This island's cuisine is the spiritual ancestor to both Cuban and Puerto Rican culinary traditions in South Florida.

The Roots of a Regional Cuisine:

New World Cuisine emerged from the rustic, resourceful kitchens of the Caribbean. It's a cuisine born of necessity, guided by ingenuity, and deeply rooted in African, Spanish, and native island traditions. These meals were built from whatever the land and sea provided: vegetables and tubers pulled from the earth, fresh seafood plucked from the ocean, poultry and pork raised close to home.

In these kitchens, nothing was wasted. Cooking was about making the most of what you had. Every part of the animal was used. Recipes were handed down through generations—not written in books, but woven into daily life.

There were no shrink-wrapped, pre-chopped onions in the local shops. Until recently, there were no canned tomatoes or ready-roasted chickens. Everything was fresh, often grown in a garden steps from the back door. If Grandma didn't pick it that morning, it didn't make it onto the dinner plate that night.

Local farmer's markets weren't just places to shop—they were social centers, places of heritage. These rustic, open-air bazaars remain one of the last connections to an authentic island food culture. That farmer selling mangoes might be your neighbor. That woman with the yams could be the matriarch of the village. This intimacy, this tryst between people and food, still thrives in the Caribbean—and South Florida chefs strive to keep that spirit alive in their own kitchens.

Culinary Finesse & Cultural Progression
Finesse in the Tropics

The Sea's First Voice:

Seafood in tropical cuisine represents simplicity and immediacy. In the Caribbean, "fresh" isn't a marketing word—it's a way of life. It means just-caught, minutes from ocean to oven, with no time for fuss or overthinking.

I've watched rickety, sun-bleached boats unload wheelbarrows of lobster straight into kitchens, where they're cooked without hesitation or reservation. No garnishes to hide behind, no heavy sauces to distract—just the natural sweetness of shellfish, honored in its prime.

That is finesse. The artistry lies not in manipulation but in restraint. True mastery is knowing when the sea has already done the work, and when the chef's role is simply to step back and let the ocean speak.

Production: A Culinary Evolution:

The "Old World" cookery traditions—rigid, hierarchical, and technique-focused—have been gradually replaced in South Florida by a freer, globally influenced culinary identity. Here, the Old World met the New and sparked a transformation. The result? A lighter, healthier, tropically driven approach now known as New World Cuisine.

Originating in the 1990s, this movement incorporated French technique with indigenous Caribbean ingredients. Over time, chefs began pulling influences and ingredients from across the tropical globe—along the same latitude as South Florida. This gave rise to a globally inspired "Palm Tree Cuisine," where mango and jackfruit meet lemongrass, yuzu, and harissa.

Today, it's not uncommon to find Japanese-Peruvian Nikkei cuisine in Miami alongside dishes built on Israeli, North African, or Southeast Asian flavors—all woven into South Florida's tropical tapestry.

The Nouveau Generation: Where It All Began:
The chefs who launched this culinary revolution were steeped in the Nouveau Cuisine tradition of the 1980s and early '90s. They plated tiny, precise portions on oversized dishes, celebrated locally sourced seafood and game, and eliminated butter and cream in favor of fruit salsas and vinaigrettes.

South Florida's abundance of tropical fruits made the transition seamless. Mango, papaya, and starfruit quickly replaced the sliced kiwi and snow pea garnishes that once ruled upscale menus. This was Spa Cuisine re-imagined—health-conscious, beautiful, and unmistakably Floridian.

Chapter Six:

Profiles of the Pioneers

Chef Allen Susser

A cornerstone of South Florida's culinary identity, Chef Allen Susser helped define New World Cuisine and elevate it into national prominence.

Named one of Food & Wine's "Top 10 New Chefs in America" (1991) and hailed by The New York Times as "the Ponce de Leon of New Floridian Cooking," Susser's imaginative French-Caribbean dishes brought serious attention to Miami's dining scene.

His 1995 cookbook, New World Cuisine, became a gospel for chefs looking to harness tropical ingredients in refined, healthy, and globally conscious ways. His evolution into "Palm Tree Cuisine"—sourcing globally from equatorial regions—epitomizes the idea of South Florida as a global food village.

Philosophy:
Rooted in classic French discipline, but elevated by the artistic use of tropical ingredients and culinary imagination. He teaches that modern food must reflect the interconnectedness of global flavors.

Chef Norman Van Aken
The only Floridian inducted into the James Beard Foundation's Who's Who of Food and Beverage in America, Chef

Norman Van Aken is credited with coining the very term New World Cuisine.

His cookbooks (Feast of Sunlight, New World Kitchen, The Exotic Fruit Book) read like love letters to tropical flavors. His early restaurant "Norman's" was considered a culinary mecca—showcasing Latin, Caribbean, and global elements in poetic, inspired menus.

Van Aken's recent projects, like Norman's 360, simplify without sacrificing soul. The once cerebral, complex plating now leans toward deeply comforting, exotically tinged fare that speaks directly to today's diners.

Philosophy:
Be special to a select few rather than trying to be everything to everyone. Speak to the cultural, emotional, and sensory experiences of your community.

Chef Cindy Hutson
A self-taught chef who began cooking at age nine, Chef Cindy Hutson channeled her early inspirations (like the "Galloping Gourmet" and "Chef Tell") into a personal Caribbean culinary language.

Her breakthrough restaurant, Norma's on the Beach (1994), was called "the best Caribbean restaurant in South Florida" by USA Today and the New York Times. Her Coral Gables follow-up,

Ortanique, expanded her focus into broader Island-Urban Fusion with hints of Asia and South America. Now with a second outpost in Grand Cayman, Hutson's cuisine has become a masterclass in fusing rural Caribbean cookery with urban sophistication.

Philosophy:
Take the soulful, rustic dishes of the Caribbean and give them a Miami polish—removing the constraints of tradition without losing authenticity.

Chef Dewey LoSasso
A Culinary Institute of America graduate and founding member of the famed "Mango Gang," Dewey LoSasso helped elevate South Florida's cuisine from casual beach eats to gourmet experience.

His Florida Progressive style first drew attention at the exclusive Foundlings Club and later as Donatella Versace's personal chef. After stints with China Grill Management in both Miami and New York, he returned to South Florida, taking over The Forge and revitalizing it with tropical, globally inspired innovation.

Philosophy:
Reinvent what haute cuisine can be—taking serious flavors and making them approachable, flavorful, and fun.

Chef Jan Jorgensen

Classically trained in Europe, Chef Jan Jorgensen fell in love with cooking at 16. After apprenticing in Europe and working with California culinary legend Jeremiah Tower, he returned to Miami to open Two Chefs in 1994—now one of South Florida's longest-running fine dining establishments.

His menus evolved with Miami's ever-changing demographics, absorbing French Nouveau, New World Cuisine, and Palm Tree Cuisine into one versatile, enduring vision.

Philosophy:

Let the menu reflect the people. Stay nimble and tuned to your city's pulse.

Chef Jan's Vision: A Fusion of Palm Tree Cuisine and Global Flavors

Chef Jan's approach to cooking is a perfect balance of tradition and innovation. His cuisine spans a wide array of influences, brought together under the concept of Palm Tree Cuisine—a culinary style rooted in the equatorial regions where palm trees thrive. This genre embraces the balance of vibrant, tropical flavors, blending classic European techniques with the freshest seafood of South Florida.

His artistry in plating and execution reveals a sophisticated understanding of both European refinement and local ingredients, making each dish not only a meal but a story on the plate. The third generation of chefs like Jan are looking beyond just culinary skills—they are finding their identity through the merging of global food sources, cooking techniques, and cultural heritage. This new generation has dug deep into their roots, recalling the lessons of the past while forging a culinary future shaped by innovation and tradition.

As Chef Jan reflects, "We lost our way when we abandoned the foundational flavors that made Florida's cuisine unique. It was like the counterculture of the 1970s—if it felt good, do it! But now, we are reclaiming the essence of Florida's culinary heritage, while infusing it with global influences that reflect the modern world."

The Randazzos: A Culinary Duo with a Global Touch

Andrea and Frank Randazzo's journey in the culinary world is as dynamic as the flavors they create. Andrea, originally from Vero Beach, Florida, was raised in an Italian family and honed her craft at the prestigious Culinary Institute of America. After meeting Frank in the kitchen, the two embarked on a shared culinary journey, and together, they've raised a family while building a legacy of gastronomic excellence.

Their careers flourished in the kitchens of Miami after years working in New York, and they've earned a reputation for crafting an eclectic American cuisine inspired by their Italian-American roots. Frank and Andrea's menus reflect their multicultural influences, each dish a reflection of their shared heritage with a twist of Mediterranean, Asian, and Southwest flavors.

A Flavorful Journey Around the World

The Randazzos have a unique ability to marry the flavors they cherish, blending the lessons passed down from their parents with international influences. What began as a homage to their Italian roots has evolved into a truly innovative approach to multicultural cooking. Their menus take diners on a journey—much like a round-the-world trip—drawing inspiration from Asia to the American Southwest, with a touch of Mediterranean warmth.

Finesse in Every Bite.

Andrea, once a Bravo Television star, has honed her culinary prowess, ensuring that every dish on the menu reflects the avant-garde finesse they've become known for. By using the finest, freshest ingredients and applying classical cooking techniques, the Randazzos bring an unparalleled depth of flavor to each plate. Their fusion of Mediterranean, Asian, and Southwest influences excites the palate with both familiar tastes and bold new combinations—each dish a testament to their creativity and dedication to culinary excellence.

Chef Michael Bloise: A Journey Through Culinary Traditions and Innovation.

Chef Michael Bloise's culinary journey is a fusion of French classical training, bold Asian influences, and deep Italian roots, all woven into the fabric of South Florida's vibrant food culture. Born into an Italian family, Michael's early exposure to simple, protein-scarce family meals sparked his drive for culinary innovation. His unique approach combines bold, Mediterranean flavors with the clean, precise techniques of Asian cuisine, resulting in a dynamic and evolving cooking style that reflects his diverse upbringing.

Culinary Education and Mentorship.

After graduating from Johnson & Wales University, Chef Michael's career blossomed through the mentorship of industry giants like Chef Frank Randazzo. Chef Randazzo's guidance, particularly on navigating the South Florida food scene, became invaluable. As Michael worked alongside Frank, he learned to adapt his menu offerings to resonate with the local palate—an essential skill that would define his future success. Chef Michael's growth as a chef culminated in his leadership at Wish, a popular local restaurant known for its innovative take on cuisine. It was here that Chef Michael truly made his mark, earning praise for his bold reinterpretations of classic Italian dishes, influenced by his training and his curiosity about global flavors. His fresh approach to menu design drew inspiration from his family's heritage while embracing South Florida's tropical bounty.

Culinary Philosophy: Tradition Meets Innovation.

For Chef Michael, culinary tradition is the foundation upon which new ideas are built. He often reflects, "If there were no French classical cuisine to base everything else on, there might not be a destiny for the new and different." His belief is that the rudiments of modern cooking, learned through years of training, give chefs the ability to innovate without losing touch with the past. To him, tradition doesn't constrain creativity—it enables it.

Chef Michael's signature style reflects this balance. His mastery of Asian cooking techniques, such as the use of fish sauce to deepen the flavors of classic sauces, highlights his knack for blending the familiar with the unexpected. He's constantly evolving, always striving to "make it better," while staying grounded in the fundamentals of classical cookery.

Creating a New Wave of Culinary Pleasure

The essence of Chef Michael's cooking is about experiences—pleasure-driven dining, not conformity. His aim is to create meals that evoke joy, comfort, and connection. "The pleasure to be experienced" is at the heart of his approach. His philosophy of cooking and dining emphasizes simplicity and authenticity, a lesson instilled by his mother, who taught him to cook with humility and focus on quality, not excess.

Now, Chef Michael has transitioned from leading large kitchens to a more intimate approach with his guests. The communal, family-oriented nature of his current culinary endeavors brings him the greatest joy. It's not about grandeur or tradition—it's about connecting with people and sharing in the pleasure of good food, simply prepared.

The Culture of Cuisine

Chef Michael believes that the true spirit of cooking lies in the "Culture of Cuisine"—a celebration of taste, tradition, and innovation. His cooking transcends any single tradition; it is a reflection of his life experiences, his mentors, and his deep connection to the roots of his family's culinary history. Whether he's crafting an Italian classic with a twist or adding a dash of Asian flair to a Mediterranean-inspired dish, Chef Michael's food invites diners to experience the world through flavor.

Chef Michael Bloise: Crafting Culinary Art from Simplicity and Boldness.

Finesse in Cooking: A Personal Journey.

Chef Michael Bloise's culinary path began in the realm of upscale cuisine, but as he matured, he realized that true fulfillment in cooking comes from simplicity. Early years in high-end kitchens pushed him to embrace the art of creating meals that are bold, yet not over-indulgent. Inspired by his mother, Chef Michael learned that the richness of a meal isn't found in excessive starches but in the depth of flavors that speak for themselves. His cooking is a reflection of that ethos—assertive flavors crafted with finesse, providing satisfaction without excess.

"Bold tastes make you as fulfilled as a starch-heavy meal, if not more," he reflects. "The finesse of assertive meals brings pleasure that's different, but just as satisfying."

A Culinary Philosophy Rooted in Happiness and Experimentation.

For Chef Michael, food is not just sustenance; it's a source of happiness, a medium through which he shares his art. His approach is simple: food is a tool for experimentation, and the kitchen is his canvas. It's through this lens that he redefines

South Florida cuisine, bringing the boldness of Asian flavors into his dishes while embracing the fresh, tropical ingredients sourced locally. The sub-tropical climate of South Florida provides a perfect backdrop for chefs to explore lighter meals that don't sacrifice bold flavors.

"Here, lightness and boldness are paramount," Chef Michael says. "Our weather drives us to create meals that are fresh, bright, and packed with flavor. We avoid heavy starches, allowing the freshness of tropical fruits like mango to take center stage."

The Mango: South Florida's Unifying Ingredient

In Chef Michael's cuisine, the mango plays a starring role. Widely known as the "King of Fruit" in South Florida, the mango is a staple in the region's cuisine, often appearing in everything from savory dishes to desserts. "Mangos are so ingrained in our culinary culture that apples and oranges seem wearisome in comparison," Michael notes. Through his dishes, he channels the culture of South Florida, blending it with global influences, particularly Asian flavors, to create a distinctive style that is all his own.

Chef Chris Nealon: Mastering the Art of Beach-front Dining

Culinary Bio: Chef Chris Nealon's journey in the culinary world began in the luxury yacht and cruise ship industry before landing at the iconic Aruba Beach Café in Fort Lauderdale. With over 20 years of experience at this renowned beach-front restaurant, Chef Chris has become synonymous with South Florida dining. His leadership has steered the restaurant through its growing pains, ultimately helping it become a landmark destination known for its stunning views and exceptional cuisine.

Thought Process: The Secret to Success

Chef Chris is a master at making seafood dishes stand out, ensuring that every item on the menu is approachable and eye-catching. "Seafood is the heart of my menu, but I always want to make it something special," says Chef Chris. His customer-friendly approach has earned him a loyal following, both among locals and tourists. With 300 seats and a bustling dining room, Aruba Beach Café thrives every day of the week, thanks to Chris's commitment to delivering what the customers want.

After two decades of providing excellent food and a great dining experience, Chef Chris has learned one key lesson: Give the people what they want, and they will keep coming back. "It's a simple thought process, but it's lost on many restaurateurs," he reflects.

"The key is listening to your customers and providing them with consistent, high-quality meals every time."

A Landmark in South Florida Dining

Thanks to Chef Chris's steady leadership, Aruba Beach Café has become a quintessential South Florida dining experience—an unmatchable combination of amazing food and breathtaking views. Chef Chris's longevity in the industry has proved that when you stay true to what works, success will follow.

Chef Chris Nealon: Adapting Classical Techniques to Florida's Lighter Side

Finesse in Cooking: A Fusion of Tradition and Local Flavor. Chef Chris Nealon's culinary career has been shaped by years of classical training, yet it is his ability to adapt to Florida's unique culinary landscape that sets him apart. After perfecting his skills in French and Italian kitchens, he discovered how to bring these time-honored techniques into harmony with the lighter, fresh style of South Florida cuisine. One of his signature dishes, the classic seafood Steamer-pot, embodies this balance—inviting diners to share a flavorful, community-oriented meal. "Classic cookery is the foundation of everything we do," Chef Chris explains. "Without it, we would have nowhere to start."

His approach to cooking is deeply rooted in his classical training but transformed by the fresh, vibrant ingredients of South Florida. Through his menus, he continually re-imagines classical dishes by infusing them with bold, tropical flavors that reflect the region's culinary diversity.

The Art of Production: Experience as the Key to Success
The kitchen at Aruba Beach Café, where Chef Chris has honed his craft for over two decades, is surprisingly small

considering the restaurant's enormous success. Despite the space limitations, Chef Chris and his team consistently manage to deliver high-quality meals that have made Aruba Beach Café a beloved local institution. "We have an old-fashioned beach-pit pig roast on the weekends, and it draws in our locals," says Chef Chris. "It's about creating an experience—a sense of community and value—that keeps people coming back."

Chef Chris's success stems from his ability to blend tradition with local flavors, all while providing a dining experience that feels personal, welcoming, and authentic. He's built his restaurant on the simple principle that when you focus on what the customer truly wants—authenticity, flavor, and value—success follows naturally.

Linda Gassenheimer: A Champion of Local, Fresh, and Soulful South Florida Cooking

Culinary Bio: Linda Gassenheimer is a well-known South Florida culinary personality, renowned for her ability to bridge the gap between professional chefs and home cooks. As a cookbook author and syndicated food columnist, Linda's work reaches over 6 million readers. Her recipes, known for their simplicity and health-conscious ingredients, help everyday cooks recreate restaurant-quality meals at home.

Linda's passion for food began during her time studying at Le Cordon Bleu in Europe, where she fell in love with French cuisine and the art of writing about food. Over the years, she has published several cookbooks, including French Cuisine, Simply Sauces, Italian Cuisine, and Keys Cuisine. Her work highlights the culinary delights of South Florida, particularly the tropical and laid-back flavors that define the region's culinary identity.

Thoughts on Modern Trends:
The Importance of Local, Fresh Ingredients.

One of Linda's key observations about South Florida's culinary scene is the rising trend of using locally grown, farm-fresh ingredients. She sees this as the best and most sustainable development in recent years. "Chefs today are turning to local farms—from the Redlands to West Palm Beach—to source their ingredients," she notes. "These farms provide the best produce, often grown organically, which is not only fresher but also better for you."

Linda's recipes reflect her belief in the power of fresh, locally sourced ingredients to create meals that speak for themselves. One of her favorites from her recent cookbook, Keys Cuisine, is a simple but stunning hogfish recipe, which balances the sweetness of mango puree with the acidity of tomato, creating a harmonious, natural flavor profile.

Finesse in Home Cooking: Keeping It Simple, Keeping It Soulful. Linda's cooking philosophy is rooted in the simplicity and warmth of home cooking. "The heart of our South Florida culinary heritage is in the simplicity of food that nourishes the soul," she explains. For Linda, the joy of cooking is in the ease of preparation and the natural goodness of the ingredients. Her family serves as her taste testers, and they always appreciate the classics—dishes that look simple yet offer deep, comforting flavors.

She loves experimenting with tropical ingredients like mango, combining them with savory spices like cumin and coriander in pork dishes. "There's something special about the mingling of sweet and savory flavors," she says. "The English were bold in their adoption of global ingredients, and today, you see similar trends in the U.S. and Europe. Chefs are experimenting with tropical ingredients, influencing the culinary landscape from France to England."

Sourcing and Cooking: The Soul of South Florida

In Linda's view, the best South Florida restaurants are those that focus on time-tested dishes and source their ingredients locally. By embracing farm-to-table practices, chefs can offer not only fresher and healthier meals but also a deeper connection to the land and the culture of South Florida.

Through her writing, Linda emphasizes the importance of creating recipes that respect the earth's natural bounty while adding her personal touch to elevate the dish.

Linda also draws on her experience in Europe to illustrate how global culinary influences, especially tropical flavors, are shaping the modern dining scene. "Even European chefs have started experimenting with tropical ingredients, and this influence is making its way into traditional cuisines," she notes. Her culinary insights have been a source of inspiration for both home cooks and professional chefs in South Florida.

Chef Alice Weingarten: A Culinary Journey of Comfort, Flavor, and Beauty.

Cookery Bio: Chef Alice Weingarten's culinary story began long before she entered the hallowed halls of the Culinary Institute of America in Hyde Park, New York. Growing up in the northern latitudes, Alice was steeped in family-based cookery from a young age, with her mother always keeping a two-pound tin of Beluga caviar in the fridge. By 17, Alice had already achieved a major culinary milestone—her carrot cake recipe was published in Gourmet magazine, making her one of the youngest contributors to the prestigious publication.

Her culinary training at the CIA laid the foundation for what would become a distinguished career in Florida. Alice's food is a mix of whimsical influences, combining Asian, Mediterranean, Cuban, and Caribbean flavors with a personal touch—often with her mother's classic meatloaf thrown in for good measure. Today, Alice's cuisine embodies her core belief that food should be comforting, delicious, beautiful, and composed of a variety of flavors and textures.

Philosophy:

For Alice, cooking is not just about creating meals—it's about sharing comfort and joy through food. Her dishes reflect this philosophy: each one is a harmonious blend of delicious flavors and textures, crafted with a personal touch that makes them uniquely hers. Whether it's a whimsical Caribbean-inspired dish or a Mediterranean creation, Alice's food is always satisfying, comforting, and aesthetically pleasing. In Key West, Alice has found a home for her distinctive culinary style, where her flavors bring people together, one delicious plate at a time.

Chapter Seven:

Not many books will tell you to go and buy another book first, but I will because it is so important to this in depth learning cycle.

The book is called CliftonStrengths finder from the ***Gallop poll***. It has been used by major corporations for years to search for the right personalities that match to certain jobs. I can tell you it has changed my life. *Here is where you can find it:*

https://www.gallup.com/cliftonstrengths/en/strengthsfinder.aspx

This is a natural lead-in to these upcoming "personal questions" from the CliftonStrengths assessment. These answers you will get after taking the test will tell you about yourself and make you a stronger person when you believe in them as I have.

Pushing Forward...

I've worked in kitchens where the heat wasn't just coming from the stove — it was coming from the pressure to perform. I've managed dining rooms where one upset guest could set off a chain reaction through the entire night. And I've seen brilliant hospitality professionals burn out, not because they lacked talent, but because they were operating outside their natural strengths day after day.

Hospitality is an industry that doesn't just demand skill — it demands the right kind of skill in the right moments.

That's where knowing your personal strengths changes everything.

The CliftonStrengths® assessment gave me, and countless professionals I've worked with, something no amount of generic career advice ever could: a clear, research-backed map of what makes us effective, energized, and irreplaceable.

Once I understood my own top strengths, I started working with my natural wiring instead of against it. I stopped trying to lead in the same way others did and started leaning into what I do best. The results were instant — higher team morale, more guest compliments, fewer late-night "fix-it" crises.

This book is for anyone in hospitality who's ready to stop guessing at their career path and start steering it with precision. We're going to break down your strengths, translate them into real-world hospitality scenarios, and give you practical tools — KPIs, worksheets, and case studies — to turn them into measurable results.

If you've ever thought, "I'm good at my job, but I know I could be doing even better", this is your playbook.

The Secret to Thriving in Hospitality

Hospitality is a business of split-second decisions and endless human interaction. Whether you're:

- A chef creating a dish under the clock,
- A hotel manager calming an irate guest, or
- A bartender juggling six orders while remembering someone's "usual,"

...success in any situation you find yourself in depends on how you think, act, and adapt under pressure.

Here's the truth:

Two people can have the same training, the same work ethic, and even the same job title — yet one thrives and the other struggles. Why?

Because their natural strengths are different.

This assessment reveals your unique patterns of excellence — the talents you naturally lean on to solve problems, connect with people, and push projects forward. It doesn't just give you a label. It gives you a ***lens*** for understanding why you excel in certain situations and feel drained in others.

When you know this about yourself, three things happen:

1. You work smarter — because you stop forcing yourself into methods that don't fit you.
2. You lead better — because you understand the strengths (and blind spots) of your team.
3. You grow faster — because you can measure, track, and expand what already works.

In hospitality, that's not just self-awareness —
that's competitive advantage.

Why This Test Is Worth Your Time?
If you've ever thought personality tests were just "feel-good fluff," let's be clear: CliftonStrengths is not that.

It's used by **Fortune 500** companies, ***world-class*** hotels, top-tier *restaurants*, and leaders across industries ***because*** it delivers actionable insight — the kind you can use to increase revenue, guest satisfaction, and your own career standing.

For hospitality professionals,
knowing your strengths means:

- You can pinpoint your value and make a compelling case for raises or promotions.
- You can tailor your role so you're doing more of what you love and less of what drains you.
- You can align your goals with your natural talents so growth feels exciting, not exhausting.

Your First Step: The Self-Discovery Questions....
Before we break down all 34 themes into hospitality-specific actions, let's start with some personal reflection questions. These will prime your mind for reading your results and connecting them to your day-to-day work.

Think of them as a warm-up before the workout — the better you answer now, the more you'll get out of this book.

Questions to Ask Yourself:

1. What parts of my job feel effortless, even on the busiest day?
2. When I'm at my best, what exactly am I doing?
3. What do my coworkers or guests compliment me on most often?
4. Which tasks or situations give me the most energy?
5. Which ones leave me feeling drained, even if I do them well?
6. If my boss asked why I should be promoted tomorrow, what proof could I give?
7. How do I naturally handle problems — with planning, creativity, people skills, or hands-on action?
8. Where in my career have I seen the biggest wins, and what strengths made them possible?

Here's the full CliftonStrengths 34 list in Gallup's official order and grouped by the ***four*** domains.

Think of each of these domains as an Index of traits that make up similar results in a persons development. (My responces are from the real world experience of over 50 years in kitchens.)

Executing Domain

1. Achiever – Great stamina; works hard; takes satisfaction from being busy and productive. (*every chef I know*)
2. Arranger – Organizes resources for maximum productivity; flexible. (*a chef has the be organized, reference: "Misen-Place"*}
3. Belief – Has core values that provide purpose and direction. (*a chef has to be believe he is doing the best job s/he can*)
4. Consistency – Treats people the same by setting clear rules and applying them fairly. (*plates have to be similar day after day*).
5. Deliberative – Careful, vigilant, private; anticipates obstacles. (*being aware new people will be your greatest challenge in the kitchen*)
6. Discipline – Enjoys routine and structure. (*sometimes taken too far*)
7. Focus – Can take a direction, follow through, and stay on track. (*director of all activities in the kitchen*)
8. Responsibility – Takes psychological ownership of commitments; honest and loyal. (*has to be the one guy that never falters*)
9. Restorative – Adept at dealing with problems; good at figuring out what's wrong and fixing it. (*daily effort*)

Influencing Domain

10. Activator – Turns thoughts into action; impatient for progress. (*what chef isn't like this*)
11. Command – Presence; can take control of a situation and make decisions. (*screams the word/title chef*)

12. Communication – Finds it easy to put thoughts into words; good conversationalist and presenter. (*sadly, many chefs lack this trait*)

13. Competition – Measures progress against others; strives to win. (*again, screams Chef*)

14. Maximizer – Focuses on strengths to stimulate excellence; prefers to transform something strong into something superb. (*chefs do what they do*)

15. Self-Assurance – Confident in ability to manage life; inner compass. (*needed*)

16. Significance – Wants to be recognized; independent; makes a big impact. (*always for any chef*)

17. Woo (Winning Others Over) – Loves meeting new people and winning them over; breaks the ice easily. (*sometimes*)

Relationship Building **Domain**

18. Adaptability – Lives in the moment; responds willingly to circumstances. (*not always, but if you can you will win the day*)

19. Connectedness – Faith in links among all things; believes there are few coincidences. (*hardly ever unless you have become a true believer*)

20. Developer – Recognizes and cultivates potential in others. (*daily challegne that has to happen at all levels in the kitchen*)

21. Empathy – Senses the feelings of others by imagining themselves in others' lives. (*sometimes, but rare*)

22. Harmony – Looks for consensus; avoids conflict. (*see above*)

23. Includer – Accepts others; makes them feel part of the

Group.(*most chefs believe as do the US Marines, you have to be born into this group or get remodeled into their image*)

24. Individualization – Intrigued with the unique qualities of each person.(*not so much for a brigade*)

25. Positivity – Has contagious enthusiasm; upbeat. (*one can only wish*)

26. Relator – Enjoys close relationships; works hard with friends to achieve goals. (*hopefull here*)

Strategic Thinking Domain

27. Analytical – Searches for reasons and causes; can see factors affecting a Situation.(*hopefully at least one chef can relate here*)

28. Context – Understands the present by researching its history. (*more and more being used to deleope the story of a menu theme*)

29. Futuristic – Inspired by the future and what could be. (*always*)

30. Ideation – Fascinated by ideas; finds connections between seemingly disparate Phenomena.(*another traits of a devlopemental chef*)

31. Input – Craves collecting and archiving; inquisitive. (*culianry-wise yes, socially-no*)

32. Intellection – Introspective; appreciates intellectual Discussions.(*another trait for the newest of our generation*)

33. Learner – Great desire to learn and Improve.(*always, everyday with younger chefs*)

34. Strategic – Creates alternative ways to proceed; quick to spot patterns and Obstacles.(*always in any sitsuation in the kitchen*)

Chapter Seven
and a Half:

Continuing on with this perspective:

To give you a real life example of this at work, ***here are my results***. Top 5 strengths (***Input, Ideation, Strategic, Restorative, Adaptability***).

Strentghts test results said this about me:

"The hospitality industry thrives on relationships, adaptability, operational excellence, and creative problem-solving. Your unique blend of strengths gives you a competitive advantage — if you know how to use them intentionally".

My results are a Hospitality Definition: *Input.*

Hospitality Definition:

In hospitality, Input isn't just about gathering random facts — it's about collecting what works in every guest interaction. A chef with Input remembers exactly which amuse-bouche wowed the bridal party last summer. A GM with Input has a binder of solved service challenges from every wedding, conference, and dinner rush.

Is it that I was born into it, or whipped into shape by 50 years of unrelenting strife and success. Maybe both, as my family has been in the business since the 1920's. At the age of nine, I first organized my brothers (7 and 5 years old) to cook sunday breakfast for my parents without any training at all. This is where I started. Many of you have similar stories I am sure.

Here is how this all works. Take the definition of the strenght and see it is real-life hospitaily circumstances.

Input strenghts:

Here are some common examples that highlight my traits in other Hospitality senerios:

Industry Actions:

1. Create and maintain a VIP Guest Profile Database — track preferences like favorite table, wine, allergies.
2. Develop a Vendor Rolodex with alternative suppliers to ensure no menu item is ever "86'd."
3. Maintain a Trend Tracker File — emerging food, beverage, and service trends you can implement first.

> *Keep a Guest Experience Journal — track specific service moments that triggered smiles, compliments, or big tips.*

Case Study:

At a luxury hotel, a maître d' with Input tracked guest anniversaries. By sending a handwritten note & dessert on each date, repeat bookings increased 22% year-over-year.

Create a Worksheet:

How to do This....create a data file to include this infromation:

- Category
- Information You Will Collect
- How You'll Store It
- How Often You'll Update
- Guest Preferences
- Vendor Contacts
- Menu Trends

KPI's....(Key Perfformance Indictors)

- % increase in repeat guests due to personalized touches.
- Average speed in sourcing hard-to-find items.
- Number of implemented trends before competitors.

Use this for Raise/Promotion Leverage:

Bring management a report showing how your guest database increased return visits, with hard dollar figures attached. This positions you as profit-generating, not just service-supporting.

IDEATION:

Innovation as a Guest Experience Engine

Hospitality Definition:

You dream in concepts. Your mind constantly connects un-related ideas to create fresh, exciting experiences that keep guests coming back because they can't get this experience anywhere else. It's the ability to connect unrelated concepts, like blending a street-food stall vibe into a 5-star rooftop lounge.

Industry Actions:

1. Develop seasonal themed menus or experiences that connect local culture to your brand.
2. Combine service elements from different cultures to create unique signature touches.
3. Propose "surprise & delight" moments that cost little but wow guests.

Case Study:

A resort bartender invented a "passport cocktail menu" — each drink came with a stamp in a collectible booklet. Guests stayed longer at the bar and increased average check size by 35%.

Worksheet:

- Current Challenge
- Wild Idea
- How It Could Work
- Next Step

Ideas into action:

- On slow Monday nights, set up a *Live* kitchen theater w/ chef. Have a Q&A with guests.
    - *Everyone loves this behind-the-scenes knowledge of cooking.*
- Pitch it to the GM

KPIs:

- Number of new guest experiences launched per quarter.
- % increase in guest spend per visit.

- Guest feedback scores mentioning creativity/novelty.

Raise/Promotion Leverage:

Document how your innovations increased guest spend or media attention, showing your role as a brand differentiator.

STRATEGIC:

Choosing the Best Path to Hospitality Excellence

Hospitality Definition:

You see the best route from A to B, even under pressure. Strategic thinkers streamline service, prevent chaos, and adapt instantly when plans change.

Industry Actions:

1. Create optimized service flow charts to reduce table turn times without reducing guest satisfaction.
2. Anticipate peak service problems and pre-allocate staff/ resources.
3. Build contingency menus in case of supply disruptions.

Case Study:

A banquet manager redesigned buffet flow to eliminate bottle-necks. Guests moved through 40% faster, freeing more time for networking and increasing positive feedback.

Worksheet:

- Situation
- Possible Routes

- Best Path
- Contingency

Into action, an Example that works:

Wine shipment delayed. Substitute local vintner's reserve. It fits the menu & maintains the quality appearance. Offer free tasting note sheet.

KPIs:

- Time saved per service cycle.
- Number of service issues resolved before escalation.
- % reduction in guest complaints about delays.

Raise/Promotion Leverage:

Present before-and-after service metrics showing how your strategies improved operational efficiency, reducing cost and guest complaints.

RESTORATIVE:

Fixing Problems Before They Damage the Guest Experience

Hospitality Definition:

You're the fixer. You spot problems quickly and have the skill to solve them — ideally before the guest even notices.

Industry Actions:

1. Audit menus for pricing accuracy, missing allergens, or supply issues weekly.
2. Develop an "Emergency Fix" SOP for service disruptions.

3. Mentor staff on identifying and solving guest dissatisfaction on the spot.

Case Study:

A front desk manager noticed a recurring AC problem in a luxury suite. Instead of comping each guest, they negotiated preventive maintenance with engineering. Savings: $12,000/year.

Worksheet:

- Problem
- Root Cause
- Fix
- Prevention

Or,

- Guest wait too long for valet
- Staff shift overlap gap
- Adjusted start time
- Added backup runner

KPIs:

- Average resolution time for guest complaints.
- % of issues resolved without manager escalation.
- Annual savings from preventive fixes.

Raise/Promotion Leverage:

Show leadership how your fixes saved costs or improved reviews, framing yourself as an operational safeguard.

ADAPTABILITY:

Thriving in Hospitality's Unpredictable Pace

Hospitality Definition:

You are calm in chaos. Last-minute changes, unpredictable guests, sudden weather shifts — you bend, don't break.

Industry Actions:

1. Master cross-training so you can step into any role in a pinch.
2. Keep a "Plan B" event setup ready at all times.
3. Maintain guest satisfaction even during high-pressure changes.

Case Study:

During an outdoor wedding, a sudden downpour hit. The adaptable banquet captain relocated the entire setup indoors in 25 minutes without guest disruption.

Worksheet:

- Unexpected Change
- Your Reaction
- Guest Perception
- Long-Term Adjustment

Into Action:

Menu item 86'd Offered VIP chef tasting plate. Felt special. Keep small-plate backups.

KPIs:

- Time taken to implement Plan B scenarios.
- % of guest satisfaction maintained during disruptions.
- Positive mentions of flexibility in guest surveys.

Raise/Promotion Leverage:

Share stories and metrics showing your adaptability saved events or preserved guest relationships, making you indispensable during crises.

Industry-Specific Action Prompts:

1. Keep a Guest Experience Journal — track specific service moments that triggered smiles, compliments, or big tips.
2. Build a Menu Memory Bank — keep notes on which dishes sell out and which flop, and why.
3. Create a Service Solution File — document how past problems were fixed (weather issues, staff shortages, supply delays).

Ideation — The Spark Behind the Service

Hospitality Definition:

In hospitality, Ideation is what keeps guests coming back — because they can't get this experience anywhere else. It's the ability to connect unrelated concepts, like blending a street-food stall vibe into a 5-star rooftop lounge.

Industry-Specific Action Prompts:

1. Host Brainstorming Tastings — invite staff to pitch and

taste-test new dishes or service ideas once a month.
2. Keep an Idea Swap Wall in the staff room where anyone can post creative concepts.
3. Test Experience Mashups — e.g., combine a wine tasting with live local art, or pair a spa package with a chef's table dinner.

Expected Results When Done Well:
* Viral guest experiences that generate free PR.
* Increased upsell revenue from unique packages and events.
* A motivated team that feels part of the creative process.

Strategic — The Playbook Planner

Hospitality Definition:
Strategic thinkers don't just have ideas — they know which ones to bet on. In hospitality, this means choosing the promotions, renovations, and menu changes that deliver maximum guest joy and revenue with minimum chaos.

Industry-Specific Action Prompts:
1. Rank all ideas by Impact, Cost, and Speed before acting.
2. Create a Quarterly Experience Map — plan key events, menu launches, and marketing pushes.
3. Do Pre-Mortems — before a new concept launches, imagine it failing and identify why so you can prevent it.

Expected Results When Done Well:

* Smooth rollouts with fewer last-minute crises.

* Higher ROI on promotions and events.

* Stronger alignment between departments (kitchen, front-of-house, marketing).

Restorative — The Service Fixer

Hospitality Definition:

Restorative talent means you spot what's broken and fix it fast. In hospitality, this is gold — from rebalancing a wine list that's not selling, to reworking service flow during a slammed Friday night.

Industry-Specific Action Prompts:

1. Hold Service Recovery Drills — role-play complaint scenarios monthly.
2. Track Complaint Patterns — fix recurring pain points before they blow up.
3. Maintain an Emergency Fix Kit — both physical (tools, backup décor) and procedural (guest comp guidelines).

Expected Results When Done Well:

* Fewer repeat complaints in online reviews.

* * Increased guest trust and loyalty.

A culture where solving problems quickly becomes second nature.

Adaptability — The On-the-Fly Maestro

Hospitality Definition:

Adaptability in hospitality is the ability to pivot when things don't go to plan — without the guest ever feeling the stress. It's what turns "We had to move the entire wedding indoors because of rain" into "That candlelit ballroom was the most magical wedding we've ever attended."

Industry-Specific Action Prompts:

1. Create Backup Venue & Menu Plans for all major events.
2. Train staff to Reframe Situations for guests — make the "Plan B" sound like an upgrade.
3. Keep Flexible Staffing Pools so you can call in extra help or shift roles mid-service.

Expected Results When Done Well:

* Guests leave impressed even when things go wrong.
* Staff morale stays high during stressful changes.
* The business becomes known for effortless problem-solving.

The Strengths Cycle in Action

Tie all five together:

1. Collect best practices (Input)
2. Create standout experiences (Ideation)
3. Select the highest-value ideas (Strategic)
4. Fix what's broken (Restorative)
5. Flex when the unexpected happens (Adaptability)

Result: A hospitality operation that's both innovative and bulletproof.

Chapter Eight:

Your Culinary Future — Building a Social Presence

The Importance of Social Media in the Restaurant Industry

Previously these ideas were nouveau, Most of these ideals are considered "of course they are needed". The revised edition of this book has so much more that is currently accepted as daily work habit.

The future of the restaurant business is undeniably intertwined with social media. In a rapidly changing digital landscape, chefs and restaurateurs must leverage the power of on-line platforms to engage with current and potential customers. The Internet is your best tool for outreach—and social media is at the forefront of this revolution.

What was once a "nice-to-have" is now an absolutely essential pillar for success. A restaurant's digital presence is as important as its physical one.

Here's a breakdown of why this is so critical and how it's playing out: The "Eat with Your Eyes" Economy: Platforms like Instagram and TikTok are tailor-made for food. High-quality, mouth-watering photos and short-form videos of dishes being prepared or plated can generate a visceral response and drive traffic like no traditional ad ever could. A potential diner's first "taste" of a restaurant is now almost always through their screen.

Building a Community, Not Just a Clientele: Social media allows for direct, two-way communication. Restaurants can respond to comments, feature customer photos (user-generated content), run polls for new menu items, and share behind-the-scenes stories. This transforms passive customers into an active, loyal community that feels connected to the brand.

Hyper-Targeted Outreach: The power of social media advertising is its precision. A restaurant can target ads to people within a specific zip code, who have shown interest in "Italian food," and are celebrating a birthday or anniversary. This level of targeted marketing is incredibly efficient and cost-effective.

The Rise of the Chef as a Brand: Chefs are no longer just hidden geniuses in the kitchen. Social media allows them to share their philosophy, their passion for ingredients, and their creative process. This personal connection makes diners feel more invested in the experience.

Immediate Feedback and Agility: Online platforms provide a real-time pulse on what customers are thinking. A restaurant can quickly see which dishes are getting the most buzz, address a negative review transparently, or promote a last-minute special to fill tables on a slow night.

When I began writing about this, social media was already growing at a rapid pace. Today, it's clear that this tool is as much a blessing as it is a challenge. The ability to reach customers directly, build a community, and share your story—without relying on expensive PR firms—is invaluable. But with great power comes great responsibility. Keeping up with ever-evolving platforms is time-consuming, which brings us to the curse: the need for continuous engagement.

The solution? Have the right team in place to manage your social media presence. It's not a one-man job. As your restaurant grows, you might need to hire a dedicated social media manager—or even multiple staff members—to keep your messaging fresh, engaging, and aligned with your brand.

That's the critical operational insight. Treating social media as an afterthought to be handled by an already over-extended chef or manager is a recipe for failure. It's a professional role that requires a specific and diverse skill set.

Hiring a dedicated manager or a small team moves a restaurant from simply having a social media presence to actively leveraging it. Here's what that dedicated resource brings to the table:

Consistency is Key: A social media manager ensures a steady stream of high-quality content. They create content calendars, schedule posts for optimal engagement times, and prevent the dreaded "ghost town" feed that hasn't been updated in weeks.

The Voice of the Brand: They are responsible for crafting and maintaining a consistent tone. Is the restaurant fun and casual? Upscale and elegant? They ensure every caption, comment, and reply reflects that brand identity.

Proactive Engagement: Instead of just posting, they actively engage. This means responding to every comment, seeking out and re-sharing customer posts, answering DMs about reservations or menu questions, and managing online reviews. They are the digital host for the restaurant.

Strategic Content Creation: It's not just about snapping a picture of the daily special. A dedicated manager thinks strategically about content pillars:

Food & Drink: *Stunning visuals of the final product.*

- *Behind the Scenes:* The kitchen in action, sourcing from a local farm, a bartender developing a new cocktail.
- People & Culture: Spotlights on the staff, from the head chef to the beloved server.
- Ambiance & Experience: Capturing the unique vibe and atmosphere of the dining room.
- Data-Driven Decisions: A professional will analyze the metrics. They know which posts drive the most engagement, what time of day their audience is most active, and how to interpret the data to refine the strategy for better results.

Social Media Channels: The Basics

There are countless social media platforms to choose from, and some are more effective than others depending on your target audience. Here's a list of must-have platforms for any chef or restaurateur:

Facebook | Instagram | Twitter | YouTube
Yelp | LinkedIn | Pinterest | TikTok

Each platform serves a unique purpose, and your restaurant should have a presence on the ones most relevant to your audience. But remember: social media is not just about broadcasting your own content. It's about engaging with your customers and creating meaningful conversations.

Becoming More Social: Moving Beyond Traditional Marketing

In the early stages of social media marketing, many restaurant marketers focus solely on message distribution—posting content that only promotes their business. This "one-way" communication is akin to placing an advertisement in the local newspaper, but it misses the mark. It doesn't allow for the kind of personal interaction that builds loyalty and connection.

The Shift: From Broadcasting to Community Building.

The core mistake is viewing social media as a free billboard. The goal isn't just to accumulate followers; it's to cultivate a loyal community. This community will not only patronize your restaurant but will also become your most powerful marketing asset through word-of-mouth and user-generated content.

Strategies for Genuine Social Interaction.

Here are actionable ways for a restaurant to be truly "social" online:

1. Ask, Don't Just Tell.

Instead of just posting "Our special tonight is salmon," engage your audience.

* Poor (Telling): "Come try our new seasonal cocktail!"
* Excellent (Asking): "We're perfecting a new fall cocktail. Should we go with a cinnamon-spiced apple base or a classic pumpkin spice? Vote in the comments!

2. Go Behind the Scenes.

People connect with people, not just logos. Humanize your brand by showing the magic behind the curtain.

Content Ideas:

* A short video of your chef enthusiastically explaining the local produce that just arrived.
* A "Meet the Team" Monday post featuring a friendly server or bartender.
* A time-lapse of the kitchen prepping for the dinner rush.
* The story behind a family recipe that's on the menu.

3. Champion User-Generated Content (UGC).

Your customers are already your best photographers and promoters. Encourage and celebrate them.

How to do it:

* Create a unique, memorable hashtag (e.g., #GoodEatsAtGinos) and display it in your restaurant.
* Regularly re-post the best customer photos to your stories and feed (always ask for permission and give credit!).

* Run a "Photo of the Month" contest where the winner gets a gift card. This incentivizes high-quality content about your business.

4. Provide Value Beyond the Plate.
Become a resource for your followers, not just a vendor.

Examples:
* Share a simplified recipe for a popular sauce or dressing.
* Offer quick tips, like "How to Pair Wine with Spicy Food."
* Highlight other local businesses or suppliers you love. This builds goodwill and positions you as a community hub.

5. Engage in Real-Time Conversation.
The "social" part is a two-way street. Your responsiveness matters.

Best Practices:
* Reply to comments and questions promptly and personally. Don't use canned responses.
* Acknowledge and thank people for positive reviews.
* Address negative feedback publicly and politely, then offer to resolve the issue offline. This shows you care and builds trust with everyone watching.

The Payoff: Why It Works
By moving beyond one-way promotion, a restaurant achieves far more than just "getting the word out." This approach:
Builds a Moat Around Your Business: A loyal community is

a powerful defense against competitors. These customers come for the connection, not just the food.

Creates Brand Advocates: Happy, engaged followers become volunteer marketers who recommend you to their friends and family with genuine enthusiasm.

Increases Customer Lifetime Value: A customer who feels a personal connection is more likely to return, celebrate special occasions with you, and forgive a minor service slip-up.

Provides Invaluable Feedback: The comments and conversations are a direct line to your customers' minds, offering real-time insights into what they love and what could be improved.

To get real value from social media, treat it less like advertising and more like hospitality. Don't just post specials—talk to people. Respond to comments, ask questions, invite opinions.

Show them what happens beyond the dining room. A cook plating the night's first order, a fish delivery hitting the counter, the pastry chef torching sugar for crème brûlée. These glimpses build trust because they feel personal.

The goal isn't a one-way broadcast. It's a conversation. When guests feel heard and included, they're more likely to return—not just for the food, but for the connection.

Tips for Building a Social Media Strategy:

Decide What You Stand For: Every restaurant has a niche, whether it's seafood, farm-to-table, or gluten-free. Define your niche early and use social media to highlight what makes your restaurant unique.

Here are five examples of how restaurants can define and showcase their niche on social media:

Farm-to-Table Restaurant:

Posts daily photos of the chef visiting local farms at sunrise, highlighting relationships with specific farmers by name. Shares "field to fork in 24 hours" stories showing vegetables being harvested in the morning and served on plates that evening. Creates weekly "Meet Your Farmer" video series featuring the people who grow their ingredients.

Authentic Regional Cuisine (e.g., Sicilian):

Shares videos of the nonna (grandmother) hand-rolling pasta using techniques passed down through generations. Posts photos of ingredients imported directly from Sicily with stories about their origins. Creates content around traditional feast days and regional celebrations, educating followers about cultural significance while showcasing authentic dishes.

Sustainable Seafood Restaurant:

Partners with local fishermen to document the daily catch, showing the boat-to-table journey. Shares educational content about seasonal fish availability and sustainable fishing practices. Posts "Ocean Report" updates explaining why certain fish aren't available during specific times, turning sustainability into engaging storytelling.

Plant-Based Fine Dining:
Creates visually stunning time-lapse videos of intricate vegetable preparations that rival any meat dish in complexity. Shares "ingredient spotlight" posts featuring unusual vegetables and how they're transformed into elegant presentations. Documents the creative process of developing plant-based versions of classic dishes.

Late-Night Comfort Food Joint:
Embraces the "cure for your midnight cravings" identity with posts timed for when people are actually craving comfort food. Shares customer stories about late-night study sessions fueled by their food. Creates content around being the "hero" for shift workers, insomniacs, and night owls who need quality food at unconventional hours.

Engage with Your Audience:
Social media should feel like a two-way conversation. Reply to messages, comment on posts, and share content that resonates with your followers.

Stay Consistent:
Regular updates keep your audience engaged. Consistency is key to building a strong on-line presence, so post regularly—but make sure the content is always relevant and high-quality.

Incorporate User-Generated Content:
Encourage your customers to share their dining experiences and tag your restaurant. User-generated content is one of the most powerful forms of social proof and builds trust.

Leverage Visuals:
Food is inherently visual, so make sure your social media posts are eye-catching. High-quality images and videos will engage your followers and showcase your restaurant's personality.

The Future of Social Media for Restaurants:
Restaurant social media is evolving beyond simple food photos and promotional posts. Within the next two years, successful restaurants will leverage AI-powered content scheduling, integrate augmented reality menu previews, and use predictive analytics to post content when their specific audience is most likely to order. The restaurants thriving in 2026 will be those who start adapting these emerging tools today. Your social media strategy now directly impacts your bottom line—restaurants with active, engaging social presence see 23% higher revenue than those without. But the bar keeps rising. Customers expect real-time responses, behind-the-scenes transparency, and personalized experiences that make them feel like insiders, not just diners.

The opportunity window is closing fast. Every month you delay building authentic connections online, competitors are capturing your potential customers' attention and loyalty. Start by choosing one platform where your ideal customers spend time, then commit to posting consistently for 90 days. Focus on showing your restaurant's personality through your team, your process, and your story—not just your plates.

The restaurants that will dominate tomorrow's market are the ones building genuine relationships with customers today. Your next post could be the one that turns a casual scroller into a regular customer. What story will you tell them?

Targeting the Right Customer Persona's:
When writing your content, make sure it aligns with the people you're trying to reach. Customer personas—which represent your ideal audience—should guide your content strategy. For example, content for a family-focused restaurant will differ from a trendy, upscale venue targeting millennials.

Content strategy should include:
Targeted messaging:
Use language that appeals to your ideal customers' needs and interests.
Engagement-based content:
Ask questions, create polls, and share interactive content to get people talking and engaging.

Call to action (CTA):
Whether it's booking a reservation or signing up for a newsletter, always include a clear CTA.

By understanding the different persona, you can tailor your content to what will resonate most with your target audience. Make sure your social media voice speaks directly to their desires and pain points.

Creating Engaging and Shareable Content:
To establish yourself as a leader in your niche, your content must be more than just promotional. Engaging content is what gets shared, and share-ability is a key driver of visibility. Your followers should feel compelled to engage with your content, whether it's liking, sharing, or commenting.

Effective content ideas include:

- Behind-the-scenes looks:
- Show how dishes are made or the story behind your ingredients.
  User-generated content:
- Encourage customers to share their experiences and tag your restaurant.
- Promotions and giveaways:
- Offer special deals that incentivize social sharing (e.g., "Share this post and get a free dessert!").

The goal is to cultivate a community, not just a customer base. As followers engage with your content, they help you build social proof and increase the likelihood of new customers discovering your brand.

Designing a Social Media Strategy:

A Win-Win....Integrating social media into your marketing strategy involves finding a balance between generating engagement and increasing sales. While social media can certainly help drive traffic and conversions, it's also about building relationships that turn into long-term loyalty.

Brand storytelling: Tell the story of your restaurant's history, mission, and values. Let your customers see the personality behind your business.

Engagement and loyalty programs:

Offer incentives for engaging with your social media (e.g., "Check in on Facebook and get a discount!").

Event promotions:

Highlight events, new menu items, or seasonal specials on your platforms.

Remember, this is a long-term play. Your efforts won't yield instant dramatic returns, but over time, as your social media presence grows, so will your brand awareness and customer loyalty.

<u>Shifting Priorities: Social Media vs. Paid Media:</u>

As the digital landscape continues to evolve, it's essential to reassess where your marketing dollars are going. For many restaurants, reallocating budget from traditional print advertising to social media engagement can yield significantly better returns—often at a lower cost.

Print Media: Still Present, But Fading.

While print advertising has long been a staple in restaurant marketing, its impact is waning in an increasingly digital world. Traditional media lacks the targeting precision and real-time analytics offered by online platforms.

The Case for Social Media:

Social media platforms like Facebook and Instagram offer highly targeted advertising options. You can reach potential customers based on specific demographics, interests, behaviors, and location. This makes your campaigns not only more effective, but also more measurable.

How to Maximize Your Targeted Advertising:

Start with Location-Based Targeting. Set your radius to 3-5 miles around your restaurant for daily specials, but expand to 10-15 miles for special events or weekend promotions. Use "people who live in this location" rather than just "people currently in this location" to capture residents who will return, not just tourists passing through.

Layer Your Demographics Strategically:

Combine age ranges with income levels and interests for precision targeting. For example, target 25-45 year olds interested in "organic food" and "local business" within your delivery radius for a farm-to-table promotion. Test different combinations and track which demographics actually convert to reservations.

Use Behavioral Targeting for Timing:
Target “frequent restaurant goers” during their decision-making windows—typically Tuesday through Thursday for weekend planning. Reach “business travelers” on Monday and Tuesday when they’re researching dinner options for their upcoming trips.

Track Beyond Clicks:
Set up Facebook Pixel to track actual reservations, online orders, and phone calls generated from your ads. Monitor cost-per-reservation rather than just cost-per-click. Create custom audiences from website visitors to retarget people who browsed your menu but didn’t book.

Test Creative Against Your Audience:
Show different creative to different segments—highlight your bar to 21-35 year olds on Thursday-Saturday, but emphasize family dining to 35-50 year olds with children. Use video content for younger audiences and high-quality food photos for older demographics who prefer static images.

Smart Budget Reallocation
By shifting a portion of your print media spend to social media:
* You gain greater reach and flexibility
* You enjoy real-time performance tracking
* You encourage higher customer interaction and engagement

Social media isn't just a trend—it's a strategic move. Investing in the right platforms can help you connect with your ideal audience and grow your brand more efficiently.

How Chefs Can Use Customer Engagement to Advance Their Careers:

Build Your Personal Culinary Brand:
Encourage customers to tag you personally (not just the restaurant) in their posts by introducing yourself tableside and sharing your Instagram handle. Offer to personally respond to reviews that mention your specific dishes. This creates a portfolio of customer testimonials tied directly to your name, which becomes invaluable when seeking head chef positions or opening your own restaurant.

Document Your Signature Creations:
Incentivize customers to post photos of your special dishes by offering a "Chef's Table experience" to the best food photo each month. Ask customers to use a hashtag with your name (#ChefMikeCreates) when posting about dishes you personally created. This builds a searchable archive of your culinary work that potential employers, investors, or media can easily find.

Create Educational Content Opportunities:
Offer cooking tips or recipe cards in exchange for social media follows, positioning yourself as both chef and educator. Host Instagram Live cooking demonstrations for customers

who've dined with you recently. This establishes your expertise beyond just cooking—showing you can teach, present, and connect with audiences.

Network Through Customer Connections:
Ask satisfied customers to connect with you on LinkedIn, especially if they work in hospitality, food media, or restaurant investment. Offer exclusive "behind the scenes" kitchen tours to customers who bring industry connections. Many career opportunities come through customer referrals, and social media makes it easier to maintain these relationships long-term.

Build Media and Influencer Relationships:
When food bloggers or local media personalities dine with you, personally ensure their experience is exceptional, then ask them to tag your personal social accounts alongside the restaurant's. Offer exclusive interviews or cooking demonstrations to food influencers who've posted about your dishes. These relationships often lead to features in food publications, TV appearances, or cookbook opportunities.

Prepare for Future Ventures:
Every positive review mentioning your name becomes social proof when you're ready to launch your own restaurant, apply for chef competitions, or seek investors. Create a "customer testimonial" highlight reel on your personal Instagram featuring people praising your specific dishes and cooking style—this becomes your career portfolio that travels with you regardless of where you work.

Incentive examples:
"Leave a review and get 10% off your next meal."
"Like us on Facebook and get a free appetizer."

The key is making it easy for customers to participate and incentivizing them with things they care about—whether it's discounts, freebies, or exclusive offers.

Measuring Success: Track Your SEO & Social Media Progress.
Tracking your digital marketing performance is essential to understanding what's working—and what's not. By setting clear, measurable goals and leveraging analytics tools, you can evaluate the impact of your social media and SEO efforts, and make informed decisions to optimize results.

Key Performance Indicators (KPIs) to Monitor:
* Engagement Metrics
Track likes, shares, comments, mentions, and saves across your platforms. These indicate how well your content resonates with your audience.
* Website Traffic

Use tools like Google Analytics to monitor traffic generated from social media. Pay attention to referral sources, session duration, and bounce rates to gauge quality of visits.
* Conversion Rates

Go beyond engagement by tracking actions such as:

* Online reservations
* Newsletter sign-ups
* Menu downloads
* Online orders

These conversions reflect the real impact of your campaigns on customer behavior and revenue.

* Optimize and Adapt

Once you have reliable data, use it to refine your approach:

* Double down on content that performs well

Adjust your targeting for better audience reach

*Experiment with posting times and ad formats

With a strategic, data-driven approach, social media can become a powerful engine for customer acquisition, loyalty, and long-term growth for your restaurant.

SEO Fashioning: Optimizing for Search Engines

When optimizing your social media content for SEO, it's crucial to align your keywords with your customer's search intent. For instance, if someone is searching for "restaurants in South Florida," make sure the words "South Florida" and "restaurant" appear naturally within your content.

To improve search engine ranking, incorporate relevant keywords into:

* Social media posts

* Hashtags
* Blog content
* Meta descriptions
* Profile bios

This SEO optimization ensures that when customers search for specific terms related to your restaurant, your content appears higher in search results. This keyword-driven strategy increases your chances of being discovered by new potential customers, especially when they are actively looking for your type of restaurant.

Conclusion: The Road to Social Media Success

Incorporating SEO strategies into your social media marketing can make a huge difference in how well your restaurant is found online. With the right content strategy, social media engagement, and SEO practices, you can significantly increase your brand's visibility and customer loyalty. Always stay engaged, track your results, and continuously optimize your content to keep up with the evolving digital landscape.

How Chefs Can Use SEO to Advance Their Careers:

Optimize Your Personal Chef Profile.

Create a professional website or portfolio page with your name as the domain (chefyourname.com). Include keywords like "executive chef [your city]," "fine dining chef," or your specialty cuisine. Write detailed descriptions of your signature dishes, culinary philosophy, and career achievements. This ensures when restaurants or recruiters search for chefs in your area, your profile appears prominently.

Claim and Optimize Your Google Knowledge Panel:
Search for your name on Google—if you don't have a knowledge panel yet, create detailed profiles on culinary websites, LinkedIn, and industry directories. Include your current restaurant, specialties, awards, and high-quality professional photos. When food writers or potential employers Google your name, they'll see a comprehensive professional snapshot.

Build Authority Through Content Marketing:
Start a food blog or contribute guest articles to culinary websites using keywords related to your expertise ("sustainable seafood techniques," "molecular gastronomy basics"). Share recipes, cooking tips, and industry insights. This positions you as a thought leader and helps you rank for searches related to your specialties.

Leverage Local SEO for Recognition:
Ensure your name appears in local restaurant reviews and food blog coverage by building relationships with food writers and bloggers. Ask them to mention you by name when reviewing your restaurant. Search for "best chefs in [your city]" and work to get featured on those lists by reaching out to local food publications.

Optimize for Industry-Specific Searches:
Include culinary school credentials, certifications, and competition wins on all your online profiles. Use industry keywords like "James Beard nominee," "Michelin-trained," or "CIA graduate" that recruiters commonly search for. Create content

around trending culinary topics to show you're current with industry developments.

Document Your Career Journey:

Maintain an updated online portfolio showcasing your career progression, signature dishes, and kitchen leadership experience. Include keywords that executive recruiters use when searching for head chefs: "P&L management," "team leadership," "menu development," and "cost control." This makes you discoverable when restaurants are actively hiring for senior positions.

Build Your Network Through SEO:

When other chefs, food writers, or industry professionals mention you online, it improves your search rankings and credibility. Engage with culinary communities, participate in chef collaborations, and maintain relationships that lead to organic online mentions of your work.

Keyword Loading: Maximizing SEO

To optimize your content for search engines, it's crucial to include targeted keywords in specific places:

Title and Heading: Include your primary keywords at the very start of your blog or webpage title and headings.

First Paragraph: The first 1-2 paragraphs should contain your keywords 3-5 times. These keywords should naturally fit into the content.

Body: Sprinkle the keywords throughout your content, ideally 2-3 times, to maintain balance and avoid keyword stuffing.

This keyword strategy is essential because search engines evaluate your content based on keyword frequency and relevance. When a customer searches for terms like "best seafood in South Florida" or "Key West dining," having the right keywords will place your restaurant's page higher in search results.

Value of Keywords: The Importance of Getting Found
Fact: 89% of people research online before deciding where to eat, especially when they're traveling. Tourists are likely to use search engines and social platforms to choose a restaurant. By having the right keywords—and including them in your website and social media pages—you position yourself as the top choice for that search.

Engaging Through Social Media
Social media isn't optional—it's a necessity. Engaging with your customers on social media platforms is now the most effective way to market your restaurant. The best part? It's free! Platforms like Facebook, Instagram, and Twitter give you a chance to directly communicate with your audience.

Key social media tips:
Consistency is Key: Be active regularly. Share updates, behind-the-scenes content, and engage in conversations with your followers.

Create Shareable Content: Photos, videos, and posts that your audience will want to share. Think about something fun, such as a behind-the-scenes look at your kitchen, a new recipe, or a unique local ingredient.

Calls to Action (CTA): Always include a CTA in your posts. Whether it's asking customers to leave a review, check in on Facebook, or sign up for your newsletter, encourage them to interact.

Social Media: A Conversation, Not a Monologue

Gone are the days of simply shouting ads to your customers. Social media marketing is a conversation between you and your audience. People expect to engage, not just be sold to. Here's how to make that shift:

Respond Promptly: Slow responses on social media can make your business look indifferent. If a customer asks a question or leaves a comment, respond quickly to show you care.

Ask Questions and Engage:

Show interest in your followers' lives. Run polls, ask for feedback, or invite them to share their favorite dining experiences.

Go Beyond Just Marketing:

Engage in conversations that are relevant to your audience's interests, not just your products.

Making Your Website the Heart of Your Media Strategy:
Your website should be the center of your digital marketing. Everything, from your social media posts to photos and videos, should link back to your website.

Here's why:
* User-Generated Content: Let customers upload photos of their meals, share their stories, and engage with your brand. This not only builds a community but gives your restaurant social proof.
* Post Content Regularly: Use your site to share news updates, blog posts, customer reviews, and photos. Google rewards active sites with higher rankings.
* Make It Mobile-Friendly: With more people searching for restaurants via mobile, ensure that your website is responsive and easy to navigate on smartphones.

QR Codes and the Future of Restaurant Marketing:
One of the newest trends is QR codes—small, scann-able codes that lead directly to your website or menu when scanned with a smartphone. It's easy to integrate them into your marketing:

Place QR codes on receipts, business cards, posters, and menus.

Enable mobile reservations:
Customers can quickly book a table or check availability directly from their smartphones.

Promote Special Offers:

Provide discounts or deals to customers who scan your QR code.

Don't Forget:

Social Media Integration and Reviews Matter

Your social media presence shouldn't just be about pushing your own message. Allow your fans to share their experiences.

Here's how: Encourage Reviews:

Ask customers to leave reviews on Yelp, Google, or Trip Advisor. Having positive reviews and star ratings will boost your reputation and attract new customers.

Promote User-Generated Content:

Share your customers' photos on Instagram or Facebook. Feature a "Customer of the Month" on your website or social pages.

Link Everything:

Make it easy for your customers to find you. Provide links to your social media profiles and encourage them to connect with you on multiple platforms.

<u>Key Stats to Keep in Mind:</u>

Social Media Growth: Over 44% of INTERNET users are active on social media. Platforms like Facebook are constantly growing, with 500,000 new users joining every day.

Traveler Behavior:

- 19% of travelers read blogs before going on vacation.
- 73% of travelers search for photos before booking a trip.
- 1/3 of travelers read online reviews before deciding where to eat.

These statistics emphasize the power of social media and online reviews in shaping the dining decisions of both locals and tourists.

Mobile Marketing:
The Future of Restaurant Marketing. More and more customers are using their smartphones to make decisions on where to eat. This presents a huge opportunity for restaurants. Consider these strategies:

Mobile-Friendly Website:
Make sure your website is easy to navigate on mobile devices.
Smartphone Apps:
Invest in a restaurant-specific app. You could allow customers to make reservations, view the menu, or order online directly from their phone.

Mobile Promotions:
Offer special deals or discounts via mobile alerts, encouraging customers to visit your restaurant while they're in the area.

Conclusion:

Engage, Optimize, and Convert

In the world of modern restaurant marketing, social media and SEO are the keys to standing out. Use the right keywords in your content, engage your audience through social media, and ensure your website is the center of your online presence. By making these efforts, you will build strong relationships with your customers and improve your visibility, ultimately leading to higher revenue and brand loyalty.

Using QR Codes & Smartphones to Boost Restaurant Marketing.

With the rise of smartphones, QR codes have become a valuable tool for restaurant marketing. Both smartphones and QR codes are powerful because they seamlessly integrate online promotions, social media, and customer engagement into the everyday lives of diners. Let's explore how to capitalize on these tools effectively.

Why QR Codes Matter

QR codes—those square barcodes that can be scanned by smartphones—are an easy way to link customers to your restaurant's digital content. With the rise in smartphone usage, QR codes have quickly become a must-have marketing tool for restaurants.

Facts:

In 2011, there were 73.3 million U.S. smartphone users, with 44% of them using their phones to browse the INTERNET.

QR codes can direct users to websites, videos, contact information, discount offers, and more.

Integrating QR Codes in Your Restaurant.

Here are several ways to effectively use QR codes in your marketing strategy:

QR Codes on Menus & Takeout Materials

QR codes are an excellent addition to your takeout menus or table settings. By placing a QR code on these materials, you can make it easier for customers to:

- Order again directly from their phones.
- Access your contact information without having to dial a number manually.
- Get direct links to your menu, blog, or even videos showing how dishes are prepared.

Business Cards with QR Codes:

Business cards are a great tool for word-of-mouth marketing. Adding a QR code on the back of your business card will allow potential customers to store your contact information directly onto their smartphones, which makes it easier for them to find you when they're hungry!

Creative tip: If customers put your card on their refrigerator, they'll have your information handy for when they need it—without flipping through a phone book or searching the web.

Link to Menu Photos:

Consider placing QR codes next to pictures of your menu items, allowing customers to:

* View recipe videos or behind-the-scenes footage of how the dish is prepared.
* Access the full menu online, especially if they want to make a quick decision while waiting in line or seated at their table.

Repeat Business Coupons:

Encourage repeat business by offering discounts through QR codes. Customers can scan the code for a special coupon that offers a discount on their next meal. This is an effective way to keep customers coming back.

Link to Social Media:

Use QR codes to encourage customers to connect with your restaurant on social media. For example, create a code that links directly to your Facebook page or Instagram profile, and encourage customers to like or follow you for updates, promotions, and special offers.

Harnessing Location-Based Marketing with Foursquare:

Foursquare is a geo-location service that lets users check-in to businesses and share their location with friends. As part of your marketing strategy, you should:

Reward frequent check-ins by offering special deals or exclusive discounts for users who check in multiple times or become the "Mayor" of your restaurant.

Use Foursquare badges to gamify the experience and keep customers engaged.

Facebook for Restaurants: Building Your Online Presence
Facebook continues to dominate as a platform for social media marketing. Here's how you can make the most out of Facebook for your restaurant:

Create distinct pages for different purposes:

- Sales page: Showcase menu items, daily specials, and upcoming events.
- Information page: Share recipes, cooking tips, behind-the-scenes looks, and fun content that helps you connect with your audience.
- Engage with customers by posting regularly and maintaining a conversational tone.
- Encourage check-ins and shares. Let customers know when you're offering specials or hosting events.
- Keep your page entertaining and relevant to your audience.

<u>The Future of Social Media & Customer Interaction:</u>
As social media platforms evolve, the future of restaurant marketing hinges on customer interaction rather than just one-way marketing. Content creators, including bloggers and influencers, play a major role in helping you increase visibility. Here's how you can leverage this: Partner with bloggers and influencers to promote your restaurant. 86% of people trust recommendations from bloggers and social influencers over traditional advertising.

Regularly update Google Maps and TripAdvisor with accurate information, because 73% of travelers use these platforms to research dining options before visiting a location.

Final Tips:

Mobile Marketing and Social Media Integration

To truly dominate the digital marketing landscape, integrate QR codes, social media, and mobile marketing strategies.

Here are a few things to keep in mind:

Optimize your restaurant's website for mobile access.

* Offer promotions through mobile apps (like Starbucks) where customers can pay directly from their phones.
* Encourage customers to share their experiences through social media, whether it's on Instagram, Facebook, or TripAdvisor.

Real-Time Media & Live Media Marketing for Restaurants

In today's fast-paced, digital landscape, restaurants need to leverage real-time media to stay ahead. Whether through augmented reality, Google tools, or RSS feeds, businesses can keep customers engaged and build brand visibility. Here's how you can implement live media marketing in your restaurant.

The Power of RSS Feeds & Content Distribution:

RSS feeds allow you to distribute your restaurant's content automatically to subscribers. By using platforms like Feedly, your restaurant can send out updates, specials, and events directly to the people who want to hear from you.

Feedly aggregates content from websites based on topics that users subscribe to. This means your content can reach people who have shown interest in similar subjects, from restaurant reviews to food trends.

Ensure your content is keyword-optimized to improve visibility. By using strategic keywords and keyword loading within your posts and content, your restaurant becomes more visible in search results.

Tip: Employ creative writers to produce content that is both engaging and SEO-friendly, ensuring it resonates with your audience while ranking well on search engines.

Augmented Reality: A Cutting-Edge Business Model: Augmented Reality (AR) offers an innovative way to enhance your customer experience by layering additional information, visuals, or videos over real-world elements.

Example: When customers open a special menu, you can overlay images or videos of dishes, customer reviews, or a chef's video explaining the dish's origins. This creates an interactive, immersive experience that could engage diners and build excitement around your offerings.

Geo-location apps like Foursquare can be combined with AR, so when customers check in, they might see badges, discounts, or personalized offers layered directly over their screen.

Google & AdWords: Restaurant Marketing Tools

To reach a larger audience, especially new customers, you need to be visible where people are searching. Google has more than 2.18 billion users daily, with 90% of customers researching restaurants online. If your restaurant isn't using Google AdWords and Google Maps, you're missing out.

Key statistics to consider:

70% of consumers decide where to eat based on what they see online.

50% search for offers or coupons before making a decision.

40% of people are specifically looking for restaurant locations.

By optimizing your restaurant's content for Google and AdWords, you ensure that your business appears in front of customers actively searching for dining options.

Tips for Keyword Optimization

Keyword loading is crucial for improving your search engine ranking and driving traffic to your restaurant's site. Here's how to make the most of it: Use keywords in your page title and headings (3-5 times in the first paragraph). Make sure the body content also uses those keywords a couple of times (2-3 times).

Focus on local SEO, such as including specific keywords like "best seafood restaurant in [City]" or "family-friendly dining [City]."

These strategies will help search engines identify your page as relevant to customer searches, improving your visibility.

Facebook: The Ultimate Social Media Platform

Facebook remains one of the most powerful platforms for restaurant marketing, particularly for engaging with customers directly. Here's how you can utilize Facebook for your restaurant:

Create different pages: One for sales, where you post menu specials, and another for information-sharing, where you share cooking tips, customer stories, or behind-the-scenes content.

Use Facebook Live to showcase events, cooking classes, or interviews with chefs. These real-time broadcasts can engage your audience, especially if you give them the chance to comment and interact during the broadcast.

The Power of Email & Newsletters

Email marketing is an effective way to maintain regular communication with your customers and keep them coming back. Monthly Newsletters: A well-written newsletter, sent once a month, can remind customers about new events, menu items, or exclusive offers.

Keep it short, engaging, and easy to read. Your customers should be able to scan it quickly and find all the essential details in a visually appealing format.

Include call-to-actions like "book a table," "order online," or "download our app" to drive conversions.

Be sure not to overwhelm your customers with emails—quality over quantity is the key.

Make Your Restaurant "Top of Mind" with Constant Engagement.
Constant engagement is crucial to staying relevant in your customers' minds. Keep the buzz alive by:
* Regularly updating social media pages.
* Sending reminders about special events.
* Offering exclusive offers to email and social media subscribers.

Don't just focus on making sales; aim to build a community around your brand. Proactive communication creates a loyal following that keeps coming back.

The Future of Marketing: Using Apps and QR Codes
Smartphone usage is growing rapidly, and integrating QR codes and mobile apps into your marketing strategy is a great way to connect with customers.

QR Codes can be placed on menus, takeout boxes, or business cards. Customers can scan them to access your menu, special offers, or social media pages.

Restaurant Apps are becoming essential. Customers can use apps for ordering, making reservations, and even paying. This gives your restaurant the competitive edge by providing a convenient and seamless customer experience.

By embracing mobile-first marketing, you can ensure that your restaurant meets the demands of today's digital-savvy customers.

Conclusion: Building a Strong Online Presence.

To succeed in today's competitive restaurant industry, you need to be visible, persuasive, and proactive. Leverage Google tools, social media, email marketing, and innovative technologies like QR codes and augmented reality to stay ahead of the competition. Make your restaurant top of mind for your customers by maintaining regular communication, offering value, and keeping the conversation going.

Maximizing Your Digital Reach: Blogs, Press Releases, and Backlinks.

In the ever-evolving world of digital marketing, creating meaningful content and leveraging the right platforms is essential for restaurant success.

This section delves into strategies for content creation, press releases, and how to make the most of backlinks to increase your restaurant's visibility.

Always Create Content for Your Blog:
Blogging is an essential tool for any restaurant looking to engage with customers and stay visible in search results. Here's how to use your blog to drive traffic and enhance your brand:

Create Relevant Content: Always ensure your blog posts are applicable and valuable to your target audience. This content should offer useful information, address common customer questions, and showcase your restaurant's uniqueness.

Use Catchy, Shareable Content: Aim to create "quote-able" content that's easy for media outlets and bloggers to share. This increases your chances of being picked up in local, regional, or national publications.

Content that Sparks Interest: Write about subjects that customers care about. Whether it's a deep dive into a new dish, behind-the-scenes kitchen stories, or seasonal ingredient spotlights, always keep the reader in mind.

Press Releases: The Power of Digital Distribution
Press releases are a great way to inform the public and media about your restaurant's latest news, promotions, or events. But how do you make sure they stand out and get noticed?

Publish Press Releases Online:
There are numerous platforms where you can publish your press release online. Google your press release afterward to see which sites have picked it up. Then, track the perfor-

mance using Alexa or other web ranking tools to see which sites perform the best.

Consistency: Use press release sites consistently to publish updates. The more often you post, the higher the chance of getting media attention, and you'll also build your online reputation.

Important Tip: Always focus on crafting a well-written release. If you're not a skilled writer, it's better to hire someone who can ensure the press release is polished and professional. Once it's online, it will be part of your digital footprint forever.

Leveraging Backlinks to Boost SEO

Backlinks are an important part of improving your restaurant's SEO (Search Engine Optimization) score. When a reputable website links to your content, it signals to Google that your website is trustworthy and relevant.

Backlink Strategy: Engage with fellow restaurant websites, foodie blogs, and local community sites. Link to their pages, and in return, request them to backlink to your restaurant's website.

Alexa Rankings: Use Alexa.com to track how well your backlinks are performing. A higher ranking means more people trust your content, which boosts your website's SEO and search engine rankings.

Effective Content Categories for Your Blog

Creating structured, focused content helps in improving the relevance of your blog. Below are some topic ideas that work well for a restaurant blog:

Crafted Cuisine: Discuss your restaurant's approach to creating a unique culinary experience. This can include cooking techniques, ingredient sourcing, or the philosophy behind your menu.

Culinary Aesthetics: Share your thoughts on food presentation and how visual appeal plays a role in the dining experience.

Culinary Passions: Talk about your personal journey in the culinary world, the dishes that inspire you, or the mentors who shaped your career.

Exotic Cookery: Introduce new, exotic flavors or dishes to your customers, showcasing how they can explore different culinary traditions.

Flavors of Florida: Given your restaurant's location, a series of posts on local Florida seafood, seasonal ingredients, or key Florida flavors will help you connect with the community.

Use Digital Platforms for Media Exposure

Social media and location-based platforms like FourSquare are crucial for visibility. They give your restaurant an opportunity to engage directly with diners.

Geo-Location Services: Encourage customers to check-in using FourSquare or Facebook. You can even offer rewards like special promotions for those who visit frequently or post reviews.

Engagement Strategy: Create engaging posts that encourage followers to share their experiences. It's not just about promoting; it's about starting a conversation and building relationships.

Conclusion: Building Your Digital Presence

The key to digital marketing success lies in consistent and targeted content creation. Focus on producing relevant blogs, optimized press releases, and backlinking to boost your visibility. Additionally, leveraging platforms like Google, FourSquare, and social media will help you stay top-of-mind with your customers and attract new ones.

INDEX:

Don't forget Michael's other books:

"Flavor Quest", "Underneath a Cloudless Sky", "All-Natural Surf Cuisine", "Interview with a Mango", "Health Choices", and "Disillusioned Malaise, Vol. 1"

....all available at www.Foodbratz.com

From Overlooked to Iconic: South Florida's Culinary Renaissance
Not long ago, South Florida was considered little more than a culinary afterthought. While the dining cultures of New York, San Francisco, and Los Angeles were celebrated as the nation's benchmarks, this region was quietly dismissed. Even the Michelin Guide—long regarded as the global arbiter of gastronomic excellence—paid South Florida scant attention.

The reason was clear: our menus once leaned heavily on convenience rather than creativity. Too often, kitchens relied on frozen fish hauled from distant oceans, prefabricated crab cakes shipped in from industrial suppliers, and bland fillets of imported whitefish that bore no connection to our own waters. The food was serviceable, but it was disconnected—disconnected from place, from story, and from soul.

What followed, however, was nothing short of a renaissance. As chefs began to reject imitation in favor of authenticity, they turned to the bounty of their own backyard: snapper and grouper still shimmering from the Gulf Stream, spiny lobster pulled from the Keys, mangoes, papayas, and avocados ripened under subtropical sun. They brought with them the culinary traditions of the Caribbean, Latin America, and beyond, fusing technique with intuition, heritage with experimentation.

South Florida, once overlooked, has become iconic—a stage where cuisine is not only consumed but celebrated, a hot style in America's ever-evolving culinary story.

Flavor Quest is more than inspiration—it's a guide, built with the careful vision of someone who knows how to turn a spark into a strategy. Every chapter moves the reader from concept to creation, from flavor memory to finished plate. Along the way, Bennett revives and restores underused techniques, breathing new life into them with tropical vibrancy. And, in the spirit of adaptability, he reminds us that great cuisine lives in motion—shaped by seasons, cultural shifts, and the personal journey of the chef.

Underneath a Cloudless Sky demonstartes Chef Michael Bennett's passion for discovery as it shines through every page. His instinct to gather stories, flavors, and techniques from fellow chefs forms the backbone of the book, creating a rich tapestry of shared culinary wisdom. Ideas flow freely, often sparked in unexpected moments—while wandering through a morning market, tasting a ripe mango, or remembering a long-forgotten flavor from childhood.

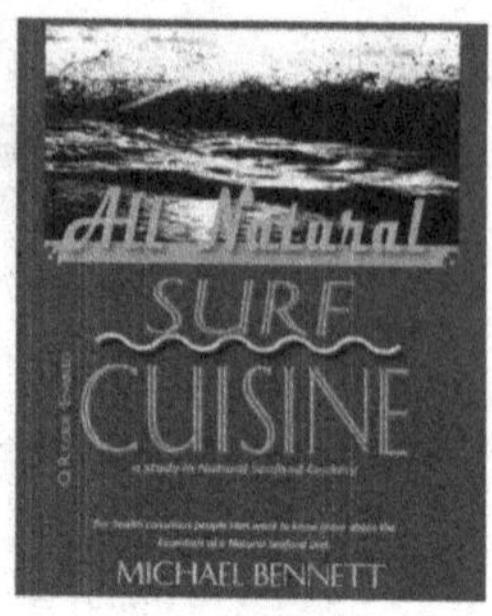

"All-Natural Surf Cuisine":

"Medi-bbean" Cuisine: He is the originator of "Medi-bbean" cookery, which emphasizes heart-healthy, gluten-free, and natural ingredients, particularly seafood. His approach aims to make healthy eating delicious and accessible. This specific cookbook is a prime example of his "Medi-bbean" philosophy, offering over 90 easy-to-prepare seafood-based recipes with a focus on healthy and natural ingredients.

Interview
with a
MANGO
Medi-bbean Cuisine
Healthy Recipes Portrayed
through the eyes of a Mango-holic Chef

Interveiw with a Mango: In today's increasingly health-conscious culinary landscape, this cookbook stands out as a vibrant celebration of nutritious cooking rooted in Caribbean tradition. The author, known for blending wholesome techniques with bold tropical flavors, brings a fresh twist to rustic island cuisine—highlighting one of their favorite ingredients: ****mango****.

Continuing a lifelong mission to educate aspiring chefs and home cooks alike, the author reimagines beloved Caribbean dishes through the lens of healthy eating. This latest cookbook is a flavorful journey that proves nutritious meals can be just as rich, comforting, and satisfying—even in culinary spaces where health wasn't always the focus.

Health Choices Is a book dedicated to cooking food that helps fight Cancer. Chef Michael Bennett is a culinary expert who has dedicated a significant part of his career to promoting healthy eating, especially in the context of fighting and preventing serious illnesses like Cancer. His emphasis on health choices largely stems from his personal experience of his wife's battle with Cancer, which he attributes these dietary changes to her recovery.

Prolific author Michael Bennett has released his latest book, ***Disillusioned Malaise***, a timely and unflinching examination of American politics and the growing frustration felt by millions of voters.

Rather than glossing over these frustrations, Chef Michael amplifies them—offering readers both a stark critique of the status quo and a rallying call for accountability. The book seeks to transform voter anger and apathy into a renewed demand for integrity, transparency, and meaningful reform in governance.

In today's media-saturated world, truth has become a casualty of political theater," Michael explains. "This erosion of trust has created a deep malaise that threatens the very foundations of our democracy. This book is my attempt to spark the honest dialogue we so desperately need.

Volume number TWO is expected Fall of 2025

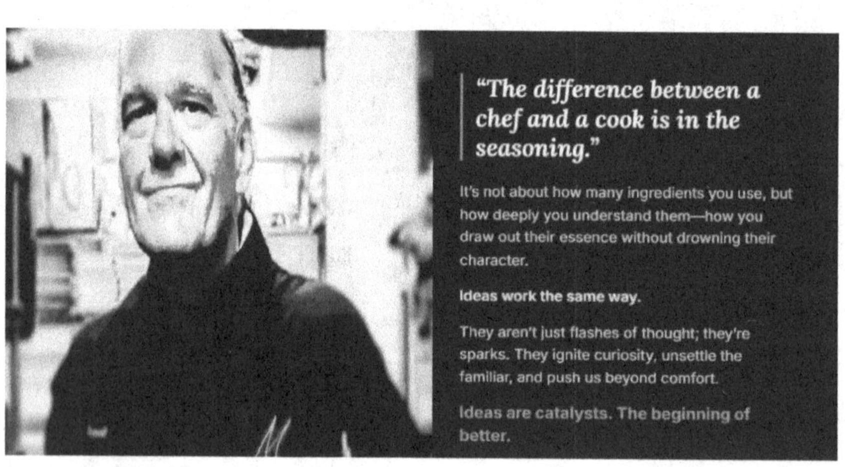
"The difference between a chef and a cook is in the seasoning."
It's not about how many ingredients you use, but how deeply you understand them—how you draw out their essence without drowning their character.
Ideas work the same way.
They aren't just flashes of thought; they're sparks. They ignite curiosity, unsettle the familiar, and push us beyond comfort.
Ideas are catalysts. The beginning of better.

www.ingramcontent.com/pod-product-compliance
Lightning Source LLC
LaVergne TN
LVHW030635080426
835510LV00022B/3374

* 9 7 8 1 6 6 6 4 1 5 1 3 1 *